Vancouver Island
B.C.
Canada ?

LAST DAYS
HANDBOOK

ROBERT LIGHTNER

LAST DAYS HANDBOOK

REVISED AND UPDATED

**A Comprehensive Guide to
Understanding the Different
Views of Prophecy.
Who believes what about
prophecy and why.**

THOMAS NELSON PUBLISHERS
NASHVILLE

Portions of this book appeared previously in *Prophecy in the Ring* published by Accent Books, Denver, Colorado.

Published in Nashville, Tennessee, by Thomas Nelson, Inc.

Scripture quotations are from the NEW KING JAMES VERSION of the Bible. Copyright © 1979, 1980, 1982, Thomas Nelson, Inc., Publishers.

Scripture quotations noted KJV are from the King James Version of the Bible.

Library of Congress Cataloging-in-Publication Data

Lightner, Robert Paul.
    The last days handbook / Robert P. Lightner. — Rev.
       p. cm.
    Includes bibliographical references and index.
    ISBN 0-7852-1250-7 (pbk.)
    1. Eschatology. 2. Millennialism. 3. Evangelicalism. I. Title.
BT821.2.L54   1997
236'.9--dc21   97-28259
                                      CIP

Printed in the United States of America
1 2 3 4 5 6 7—04 03 02 01 00 99 98 97

To
my grandchildren,
Nathan Shotts,
Jonathan Shotts,
Amanda Shotts,
Austin Bracy,
Conner Bracy,
Taryn Bracy,
Andrew Steitz,
Timothy Steitz,
Benjamin Steitz,
Caleb Steitz,
with the prayer that
they will be
discerning of
the last days

Other Books by the Author

The Savior and the Scriptures
Neo-Evangelicalism
Truth for the Good Life
Neo-Liberalism
James: Apostle of Practical Christianity
The God of the Bible and Other "Gods"
Heaven for Those Who Can't Believe
Speaking in Tongues and Divine Healing
Church Union: A Layman's Guide
The Death Christ Died
Handbook of Evangelical Theology
Sin, the Savior and Salvation

Contents

Charts and Illustrations

Foreword

Most doctrines divide or unite believers. Even such a basic one as salvation. Is salvation by faith or by faith plus some works? Depravity, security, baptism, church government, gifts of the Spirit—to name a few—also divide and unite Christians.

Differences over eschatology generate some of the more heated discussions, especially in our day. Yet, as Dr. Lightner points out, there are many areas of eschatology about which evangelicals agree.

But what about those areas of disagreement? Which millennial view is correct? Which rapture view? Dr. Lightner clearly outlines the differences and the reasons why Christians hold these different opinions, then pleads for understanding and consideration. He does not ask any to abandon their viewpoints, but to hold them intelligently and in love.

The author's emphases in this book need to be heard and heeded.

—CHARLES C. RYRIE
of Ryrie Study Bible

Introduction: Most Frequently Asked Questions about End-times Prophecy

Though written over 200 years ago, John Newton's "Amazing Grace" has lost none of its ability to touch chords deep within us:

> Amazing grace!
> How sweet the sound,
> That saved a wretch like me!
> I once was lost,
> But now am found
> Was blind, but now I see.

Something about the melody and the words is *immediately* interesting, appealing, and evocative. Regardless of whether the song reflects our sentiments and experience, it stirs the hearts of men and women around the world.

And yet the song takes on a deeper and more powerful meaning when we learn that the man who wrote the song, John Newton, spent ten years of his life in the African slave trade. Trafficking in men and treating them in ways that a good man wouldn't treat his dog, John Newton truly was a man who had done wretched things. In short, he was *exactly* the kind of man God was looking for.

God transformed John Newton, "chief among sinners," into a preacher of the Gospel—and Newton never got over the wonder of that divine transaction. And it was that sense of wonder that led him to pen the words to "Amazing Grace," setting them to the tune of a popular bar song with which he was only too familiar. Knowing the background—the story *behind* the story, if you please—increases our appreciation for the song.

Just as something about "Amazing Grace" moves people, so also something about Bible prophecy is inherently intriguing to people. From the Bible we know that God is intimately involved, not only in the moment-by-moment existence of the universe, but also in the affairs of humanity. Yet prophecy speaks of much more than this. Using vivid language and mysterious imagery, it speaks in great detail of coming times of unprecedented and dramatic destruction, devastation, and deliverance. It at once warns *and* encourages us about things to come—and enjoins us to watch expectantly for their inevitable fulfillment.

And so we are drawn to books and sermons which address prophetic issues like, "How do we understand prophecy?" "Is the destruction prophesied in Scripture the result of atomic warfare, or Ebola-like disease—or both?" or, "Who is the Antichrist?" The prophetic portions of the Word of God are as interesting as tomorrow's newspaper—and far more accurate—and so of course we want to know more.

This book is about prophecy—and prophecy is a vitally important subject. You are to be commended for taking the time to dig deeper in it. Prophecy is as timeless as God's settled Word, and as current as tomorrow's newspaper. Every tick of the clock brings God's prophecies that much closer to fulfillment. Even the most cursory glance reveals that the events prophesied in the Bible are taking shape. We see this, know the time is short, and want to know the answers to questions like, "Are we the terminal generation?" or "Is the U. S. A. mentioned in prophecy?"

These are fair questions—and good ones—and this book is going to answer some of these kinds of questions. But this book is also my invitation to go deeper—to delve into the issues *behind* these intriguing questions. Armed with this background, you understand and appreciate prophecy *much more.*

Many people would rather avoid prophecy altogether. Some keep their distance because they don't know how to distinguish between people who treat the text with integrity and those who are just as adamant that Gorbachev's birthmark is the mark of the beast. This book will answer "hot" questions carefully and textually—while at the same time giving you a crucial foundation for understanding prophecy and evaluating prophetic teaching.

Others prefer to stay on the very surface of prophecy. To them it seems that for every two Christians there are three positions on the same prophetic issue. Despairing that anything can be known for sure, they dismiss prophecy, saying, "The big idea is that God wins. The rest is detail." Well, God certainly does win. But if that were all the attention God wanted us to pay to prophecy, it doesn't make much sense that He allotted more than a quarter of the Bible to communicate what He could have communicated in two words, "God wins." This book will show you both the relevance of prophecy and its importance, regardless of the position you may hold.

With great care and conviction, evangelicals have set forth their particular views of God's program for the future. Much time and effort have been spent, and are still being spent, in defense of specific details of end-time events. It seems that as soon as a particular view is presented and defended, it is countered and answered by arguments from an opposing side.

As we will see later in this volume, those classified as evangelical (conservative, orthodox, or fundamental) have a great deal in common as they embrace the historic Christian faith. Yet they battle fiercely with each other over things to come. While they stand united when it comes to the great historic truths of the Christian faith, they are sorely divided in their understanding of God's plan for the future. Why? These pages will take you deeper to answer this urgent question.

For a long time I have sensed the need to set forth the differences among evangelicals over things to come in the hope that the study would serve to ease tensions and strengthen ties among Bible believers. We evangelicals simply have too much in common to lose to the opposition because of our differences in eschatology.

This study will set forth the major differences among evangelicals in their interpretation of unfulfilled prophecy. I have made every effort to be objective and fair in presenting the different evangelical views. It may be hard for some to admit but it is still true: no particular scheme of end-time events is without its problems. Helpful suggestions are made in this work for further reading and study in each of the various views.

The purpose of this book is not to defend my particular view of eschatology. In the section that follows, "Frequently Asked Questions about the Last Days," I will answer these questions from my own point of view, which is pretribulational and premillennial. However, in the rest of the book I will not critique the other positions on things to come, but instead will set them out as fairly as I know how.

Since this is, at least in part, a study of what evangelicals believe, it is presented on the premise that the Bible in its entirety is the inerrant Word of God. The Scriptures are viewed as the basis and guide for all doctrinal beliefs, including those concerning the future program of God.

May the One around whom all unfulfilled prophecy revolves, even the Lord Jesus Christ, be exalted in the pages and in the heart and life of the reader as we begin by looking at the frequently asked questions about the last days.

Frequently Asked Questions about the Last Days

 ## 1. Is this the terminal generation?

A very important doctrine of the Scripture is that of "imminence," which means that Jesus Christ could return again to the earth for His Church *at any moment.* So from a doctrinal perspective, I believe that every generation should consider itself the terminal generation—that is, we should live and work and pray as if the Lord Jesus were coming today.

So it is certainly possible that we are the terminal generation. But we have to be very careful about this to not set dates for Christ's return. Jesus explicitly told us "But of that day and hour no one knows, not even the angels in heaven, nor the Son, but only the Father" (Mark 13:32). We have to be careful not to paint God into a corner. Some interpret passages like Matthew 24:34 to teach that Jesus must return within one generation of the re-establishment of Israel. Yet the word, "generation," can also mean "race or ethnic group," and thus passages like Matthew 24:34 could be teaching that the Jewish people will endure despite Satan's efforts to obliterate them.

So be careful not to set dates—while at the same time being careful to live with great expectancy.

For more on this, see pages 88, 116, 228.

 ## 2. Are there any indications that Christ may return soon?

Yes. There are a number of events transpiring which indicate God is setting the stage for all that will transpire after Christ returns for His own. Perhaps the reconstitution of Israel as a nation and the computer age are among the greatest indications.

I mention Israel because it is clear from Scripture that in the end times God is dealing with Israel and the nations. Yet from the destruction wrought by Titus in the first century to 1948, the nation of Israel did not exist. So her existence today as a nation seems to indicate that the stage is being set. By the same token, it is entirely possible that the nation of Israel could be wiped off of the map to-morrow. But if this happened, and I pray that it won't, then God would have to start over again regathering Israel as a nation.

I mention computers because computer technology, its convergence with television, and its integration into the economy make it more possible than ever before for one person to control the economy, the media, and information itself. The Scripture is clear that in the Tribulation one (unspeakably evil) person will exercise this kind of control. His name will be "Antichrist."

For more on this, see page 88 and Chapter 11.

 ## 3. Is the U. S. A. mentioned in prophecy?

Not directly, so we don't know what her involvement will be in the Tribulation and the battle of Armageddon. There are a number of reasons advanced for why this should be so. Some think the U. S. A. is not mentioned in Scripture because she will no longer exist as a nation, either through war or plague or some other calamity.

Others believe that the U. S. A. will be part of the revived Roman Empire which will be headed by the Antichrist. It is also worth noting that while specific geographic locations and peoples are given for the Northern and Southern powers, they are not given for the Eastern force nor the revived Roman Empire. If the U. S. A. is a part of the Antichrist's confederation, then that means she will eventually turn against her historic ally, Israel.

For more on this, see pages 88, 95.

4. Who has a legitimate right to control Palestine, including Jerusalem, the West Bank, the Golan Heights, and Gaza?

The nation of Israel, and no one else. The potential for misunderstanding here is high, so let me explain. God's covenant with Abraham in Genesis 12 was *unconditional,* that is, God gave certain things to Abraham regardless of the behavior of Abraham and his descendants—and the land of Israel is one of those things. In fact, Israel's legitimate borders are *much larger* than what she currently occupies. God describes its dimensions in Deuteronomy 11:24, 25: "Every place on which the sole of your foot treads shall be yours: from the wilderness and Lebanon, from the river, the River Euphrates, even to the Western Sea, shall be your territory. No man shall be able to stand against you; the Lord your God will put the dread of you and the fear of you upon all the land where you tread, just as He has said to you."

Now while Israel has a right to the land, she does not, as yet, have the right to the blessing of God in the land. And just because Israel has retaken Palestine doesn't mean that her covenant with God has been fulfilled. Israel is in unbelief, and her title to the land doesn't mean that everything she does—particularly with regard to the Palestinians—is justified. As the Word talks about in Ezekiel 37, God is going to use the nations—including Palestinians and Arabs—to discipline Israel until she at last comes to believe in her Messiah and embraces God's conditions for blessing.

CAUTION! while interesting — These answers are full of Human opinions! Be cautious in agreeing outside of scripture!!

5. Will the city of Babylon be rebuilt?

I believe that a literal interpretation of the Scripture requires this. The Bible speaks of a judgment on Babylon which will result in its final devastation. Since this event has yet to occur, I conclude that it will happen in the future. And since not much of anything will be constructed during the Tribulation, that leads me to conclude that Babylon will be rebuilt before the Tribulation on its historical location in present-day Iraq.

The Babylon that will be rebuilt is different from the commercial and religious Babylon described in Revelation 17 and 18. However, the rebuilt Babylon, like the tower of Babel so many years ago, will be the center of pagan idolatry and anti-Christian activity.

6. Why is the Middle East, the Holy Land, so important to national leaders?

One part of the answer is purely geographical, for the Middle East is the nexus of three continents, Europe, Asia, and Africa. Also, world commerce flows through the Mediterranean Sea and the Suez Canal, and a large percentage of the world's oil comes from the Persian Gulf region.

Yet as important as these things are, there is much more to it than that. The Holy Land is the subject of a promise by God to His chosen people. It is the place where He brought His Son into the world. It is the place where He was crucified. It is the place from which He ascended—and to which He will return with power and majesty. Satan, the enemy of our souls, contends for anything precious to God. So Satan contends indirectly for the Holy Land through false religions and governments, and one day will contend directly through the Antichrist and the campaign of Armageddon.

 ## 7. What kingdom did Jesus say was "at hand"?

Jesus, along with John the Baptist, the twelve apostles, and the seventy whom He sent out in pairs preached the very same message. It was a bona fide offer of the Davidic, earthly, messianic kingdom. The contingency of the offer was that the nation needed to repent for the kingdom to be established. They did not repent. The kingdom "at hand" in Jesus' day is not now a reality in any sense, but it will be when He sits on David's throne in Jerusalem and rules the world with a rod of iron at His second advent. I'll discuss this in more detail in question 10, but at the end of the Tribulation, the Jewish people will turn to their Messiah, "looking toward Him whom they have pierced," and so be saved. Then, during the Millennium, the kingdom that was "at hand" will be on earth.

For more on this, see pages 133, 135.

 ## 8. Why is one's view of last-day events important?

First of all, everything God has told us in the Bible is important. Fully two-thirds of the Bible was predictive when it was written. If God deems prophecy so important that He devotes two-thirds of His Word to detailing it for us, surely we must afford prophecy the same thoughtful search that the rest of the Word deserves and demands.

And in fact when you approach prophecy thought-fully and reverently, its importance soon becomes apparent. We have no guarantee that today will be like yesterday. Quite the opposite—we learn from prophecy that there is an hour coming when God will decisively and definitively intervene in human history. In those days of divine intervention and wrath, the detailed instructions of prophecy will be vitally useful. Fully embracing these realities makes our lives distinctive.

One day believers will be suddenly snatched away from this earth, there to give an account before God for the deeds they have done. Embracing this truth will lead you to keep short accounts with God and others, to deal with sin right away, to work from a heart of gratitude for the Father. All this because Bible prophecy teaches us that believers will appear before the judgment seat of Christ to be judged for the deeds done in the body, and so receive either reward or loss of reward. I can't help but wonder whether some of those who suffer loss of reward in that day will be those who discounted the importance of prophecy and so weren't prepared for His coming.

For more on this, see pages 51–58.

 ## 9. Why did the earliest Christian writers not write about last-day events?

First of all, there tends to be an assumption hidden in this kind of question: "If prophecy was important, then surely we would find the early church addressing it in detail." And in fact the early church did not address prophecy in detail. For instance, while the Apostles Creed affirms that Jesus is coming again, it doesn't go into any more detail than that.

But just because the early church didn't teach in detail on prophecy doesn't mean that it was unimportant. You see, systematic theology is always formulated in an atmosphere of controversy. In the early church, the controversy swirled around the threeness and oneness of God and the twoness and oneness of Christ. As these issues were resolved by the church, the controversy moved on to areas like the doctrine of salvation and the church. In God's time, the church focused on prophecy and a great wealth of material on prophetic literature was produced.

For more on this, see page 85.

10. Is Christ on the throne of David now?

No. He is at the right hand of His Father's throne. Interestingly enough, David's throne is *never* pictured as being in heaven but always on earth as a physical, literal, earthly throne. David ruled over an actual geographical area, and so will David's son and the focal point of David's dynasty, the Lord Jesus.

From the right hand of the Father, Jesus is currently interceding on our behalf with the Father, and preparing dwelling places for us. But in the Millennium, the Lord Jesus will rule *from* the literal, physical throne of David in Jerusalem. He will rule over all the earth from there in a time of unprecedented peace and prosperity.

For more on this, see pages 132–135, 169–170.

11. How is Jesus going to return?

First, He will come in the clouds of heaven and gather His own who are alive on the earth. Believers who have died since the Day of Pentecost will be raised from the dead and together these will all go to be forever with the Lord. This is the Rapture. Following this coming of Christ, the Great Tribulation will take place on earth. After this, those who were raptured and raised when Christ came in the clouds will return with Him and He will establish His kingdom on earth. This is the Second Coming.

Some scholars lump the Rapture and the Second Coming together. Here's why I believe they are distinct events. While the Rapture is described as something which brings peace and comfort, and for which believers should anticipate with longing, the Second Coming is "after the Tribulation of those days," following on the heels of the great outpouring of God's wrath. In the Rapture, Christ comes to the air. In the Second Coming, Christ comes to the earth. After the Rapture, believers appear before the judgment seat of Christ and will be with the Lord forever. After the Second Coming, Christ judges the nations and Israel, and then rules from the throne of David in Jerusalem over the world. At the Rapture, Christ comes *for* His saints. At the Second Coming, Christ comes *with* His saints.

A close comparison of John 14:1–3, 1 Thessalonians 4:13–18, and 1 Corinthians 15:51, 52 with Matthew 25 and Revelation 19 will, I believe, demonstrate that the Rapture and the Second Coming are separate events. Chart 1 further illustrates the differences.

For more on this, see pages 87–89.

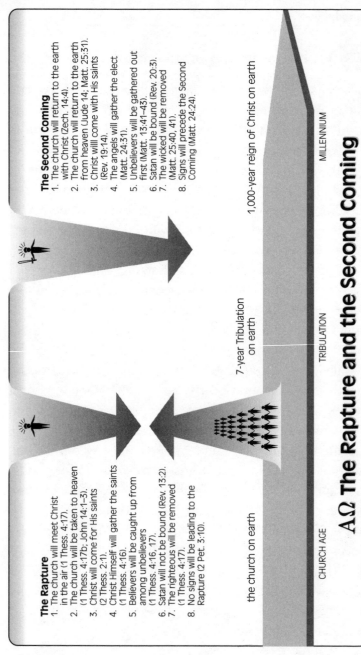

The Rapture

1. The church will meet Christ in the air (1 Thess. 4:17).
2. The church will be taken to heaven (1 Thess. 4:17b; John 14:1–3).
3. Christ will come for His saints (2 Thess. 2:1).
4. Christ Himself will gather the saints (1 Thess. 4:16).
5. Believers will be caught up from among unbelievers (1 Thess. 4:16, 17).
6. Satan will not be bound (Rev. 13:2).
7. The righteous will be removed (1 Thess. 4:17).
8. No signs will be leading to the Rapture (2 Pet. 3:10).

The Second Coming

1. The church will return to the earth with Christ (Zech. 14:4).
2. The church will return to the earth from heaven (Jude 14; Matt. 25:31).
3. Christ will come with His saints (Rev. 19:14).
4. The angels will gather the elect (Matt. 24:31).
5. Unbelievers will be gathered out first (Matt. 13:41–43).
6. Satan will be bound (Rev. 20:3).
7. The wicked will be removed (Matt. 25:40, 41).
8. Signs will precede the Second Coming (Matt. 24:24).

the church on earth

7-year Tribulation on earth

1,000-year reign of Christ on earth

CHURCH AGE

TRIBULATION

MILLENNIUM

AΩ The Rapture and the Second Coming

Chart 1

12. What is meant by the coming Great Tribulation?

This is a future seven-year period when God's wrath will be poured out on the earth as never before. It is the seventieth week of Daniel 9:24–27. Many students of prophecy refer only to the second half of this period as the "Great Tribulation." I have no quarrel with them, but the first half of the Tribulation is going to involve *great* Tribulation while the second half, if anything, is going to involve *greater* Tribulation. I think it is very important to recognize that the entire seven-year period is going to be an unprecedented outpouring of God's wrath.

The Tribulation will begin when Israel signs a treaty with the Antichrist, who undertakes to guarantee Israel's peace. Thereafter the devastating seal judgments are visited upon the earth. Around the midpoint of the Tribulation, the trumpet judgments devastate the earth, and then shortly before the Second Coming, the bowl judgments are poured out upon the earth. The effects of these judgments are lingering and compounding, and things on the earth dramatically and progressively deteriorate. The Tribulation ends with the Second Coming of Christ, who defeats Satan and the armies of the world at Armageddon, and ushers in a millennial kingdom of peace, prosperity, and righteousness. Charts 2 and 3 deal with this period.

For more on this, see pages 86, 94.

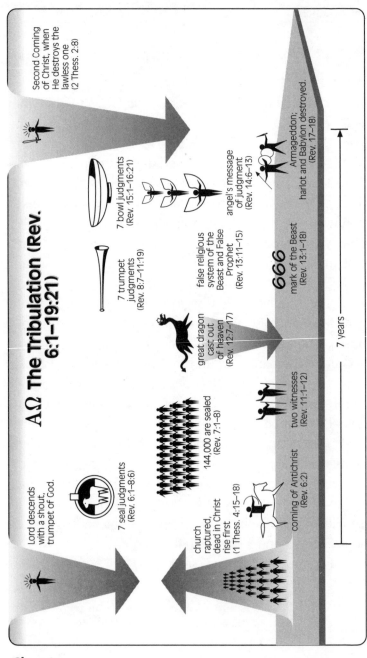

AΩ The Tribulation (Rev. 6:1–19:21)

Second Coming of Christ, when He destroys the lawless one (2 Thess. 2:8)

Lord descends with a shout, trumpet of God.

7 seal judgments (Rev. 6:1–8:6)

7 trumpet judgments (Rev. 8:7–11:19)

7 bowl judgments (Rev. 15:1–16:21)

144,000 are sealed (Rev. 7:1–8)

great dragon cast out of heaven (Rev. 12:7–17)

angel's message of judgment (Rev. 14:6–13)

Armageddon; harlot and Babylon destroyed. (Rev. 17–18)

church raptured, dead in Christ rise first (1 Thess. 4:15–18)

two witnesses (Rev. 11:1–12)

false religious system of the Beast and False Prophet (Rev. 13:11–15)

666

mark of the Beast (Rev. 13:1–18)

coming of Antichrist (Rev. 6:2)

7 years

Chart 2

ΑΩ The Seals, Trumpets and Bowls of Revelation

Seals (Rev. 6:1–8:6)

1. White horse	2. Red horse	3. Black horse	4. Pale horse	5. Souls under the altar	6. Natural, physical calamity	7. Silence
Antichrist	War	Famine	Death	Martyrdom	Fear upon all men	

Trumpets (Rev. 8:7–11:19)

1. Hail, fire, blood	2. Burning mountain	3. Star falls from heaven	4. Heavenly bodies are struck	5. First "woe"	6. Second "woe"	7. Third "woe"
1/3 of earth's vegetation destroyed	1/3 of sea turns to blood	1/3 of rivers become contaminated	1/3 of light is lost	plague of terrible locusts	1/3 of mankind is killed	

Bowls (Rev. 15:1–16:21)

1. Foul sores	2. Seas become blood	3. Rivers become blood	4. Sun becomes scorching	5. Darkness	6. Euphrates River dried up	7. Thunder, lightening, earthquake
those with mark of the Beast are afflicted	all sea creatures die	those who killed martyrs must drink blood	those burned by the sun blaspheme God	great pain inflicted on those who follow the Beast	wicked nations of the earth gather at Armageddon	God's fierce wrath upon Babylon

Chart 3

13. What is meant by "And unless those days were shortened, no flesh would be saved; but for the elect's sake those days will be shortened"?

There will be so much disruption, destruction, and death during the Tribulation, that if God allowed it to go any longer than seven years, all life would be destroyed on the earth. Remember, Satan is the great imitator. And in the Tribulation, Satan makes his play to imitate the one-world government that will exist on the earth during the Millennium. Except instead of peace, there is war. Instead of the removal of the curse, it is a time of wrath. Instead of the elongation of life, there is unprecedented death. And if God did not intervene on the earth by sending His Son along with the armies of heaven, life on earth would simply cease to exist.

 14. If we interpret the prophetic passages literally, millions of people will be slaughtered by God Himself. How does this fit with God's character?

There *will* be an enormous amount of bloodshed, and the passages which describe this only serve to amplify what the Scripture means when it says that the Tribulation is an outpouring of God's wrath. And visitations of God's wrath accompanied by bloodshed are not without precedent. When Israel was laying claim to the Promised Land, they were commanded by God Himself to slaughter all of the inhabitants of land—men, women, and children. The

Judge of all the earth *will* do right, and we must not impose upon God our standard of righteousness. Rather, we must understand the true meaning of righteousness both from what the Scripture *says* and from what the Scripture *shows*.

15. Why are church saints spared the Tribulation and so many other Christians are not?

The quick answer is: God has not told us why. Neither do we know why in the early years of Christianity so many had to die for their faith. But underneath this question is the nagging issue of the fairness of God. A sovereign God *could* prevent suffering. A loving God *would* prevent suffering. Yet there *is* suffering—so how do we account for this?

First of all, in the Scriptures, suffering isn't presented as a uniformly evil thing. The highest level of intimacy with God is "the fellowship of his sufferings" (Phil. 3:10). Heroes of faith are said to have rejected deliverance from their *torture* "that they might obtain a better resurrection" (Heb. 11:35).

Second, the Scriptures always call us back to the character of God. In the midst of a devastating passage on the judgment of nations and peoples who had been disobedient, Nahum exclaims: "The Lord *is* good, a stronghold in the day of trouble; and He knows those who trust in Him." After describing God's sovereign right to elect some to salvation and not others, the apostle Paul exclaims, "Oh, the depth of the riches both of the wisdom and knowledge of God! How unsearchable are His judgments and His ways past finding out!" (Rom. 11:33). We cannot understand His ways now, but someday we will know as we are known, and will apprehend by sight what we now affirm by faith—our God does *all* things exceedingly well.

 16. Will anyone be saved during the Tribulation who has *rejected* Christ before the Rapture?

Probably not. The apostle Paul declares in 2 Thessalonians 2:9–12: "The coming of the lawless one is according to the working of Satan, with all power, signs, and lying wonders, and with all unrighteous deception among those who perish, because they did not receive the love of the truth, that they might be saved. And for this reason *God will send them strong delusion, that they should believe the lie, that they all may be condemned who did not believe the truth* but had pleasure in unrighteousness."

In other words, it appears that God will allow them to be supernaturally blinded by Satan. This just underscores the importance for the lost who have heard the gospel to trust Christ *right now.* Not only is there no guarantee about tomorrow, but this passage seems to indicate that there is a guarantee that there will be no tomorrow if they make a conscious decision to reject the claims of Christ and the Rapture occurs.

Nevertheless, those who had not been confronted with the gospel and therefore have never said "no" to Christ, very likely *will* have the opportunity to become Christians—I believe that millions upon millions will.

For more on this, see pages 89–91.

17. Will anyone be saved during the Tribulation?

Yes, a multitude will come to faith in Christ through the witness of the 144,000, the two witnesses of Revelation 11, and those who believe. Revelation 7:9 declares, "After these things I looked, and behold, *a great multitude which no one could number,* of all nations, tribes, peoples, and tongues, standing before the throne and before the Lamb, clothed with white robes, with palm branches in their hands."

On the basis of this passage of Scripture, I believe that more people will come to faith in Christ during the Tribulation than in any other seven-year period in human history. We tend to emphasize the great outpouring of wrath so much that we may find it hard to imagine people being saved in such a time. But it is just like our God to pour out mercy, even in the midst of judgment.

 ## 18. What happens to people who *cannot* believe (as opposed to will not) at the Rapture?

There are two kinds of people who would fit into this category. The first would be those who *at one time were capable of believing.* For instance, an elderly person with Alzheimer's Syndrome, or an adult lying in a coma because of an automobile accident. These people, having failed to trust Christ while they had an opportunity to, will not be raptured, and when they die, will be relegated to Hades to await the Great White Throne Judgment.

In the second group would be those who were *never*

capable of believing—for instance, babies, infants, and those who are mentally impaired. The Bible does not explicitly speak to this, but it *does* speak about the character of God. And because of the character of God it seems to me that these people have an eternal destiny with Jesus in heaven.

The Bible does not tell us, but a sovereign, loving God gives credence to the fact that at the Rapture all infants and mentally impaired people go along with the redeemed to be forever with the Lord. Jesus died for the sins of the whole world—including infants and the mentally impaired, who cannot exercise faith in Christ. Although God calls for all humankind to come into a faith relationship with Him through Christ, there is nothing meritorious in faith, in and of itself. So I believe that God secures the eternal destinies of these people by applying the finished work of Christ to their account *for them.* And while there are no passages of Scripture which address this, there are also no passages of Scripture which explicitly put these people in hell, either. To explore this further, be sure to study Matthew 18:1–14, Mark 10:13–16, and 2 Samuel 12:22–23. I've also addressed this topic at some length in my books, *Heaven for Those Who Can't Believe* and *Sin, the Savior and Salvation.*

 19. Who will be the Antichrist?

We do not know who he is—but we are told about his character and his conduct. Because of the importance of this question, I'm going to take some time to develop it.

The Antichrist, whose signing of a covenant with Israel will commence the Tribulation, is *the* major human character in it.

John describes him as "a beast" in Revelation 3:1–15. Not only will his character be beastly, but so will his appearance. In Daniel 7:8, he is described as the "little horn" on the fourth beast, which symbolizes "a fourth kingdom on earth" (Dan. 7:23)—namely some form of a revived Roman Empire. This revived Roman Empire may only share geographical boundaries with the old Roman Empire, or it might be something much more than that.

He will not be from a monotheistic background. Daniel 11:37 refers to "the God [lit. "gods"] of his fathers." This seems to indicate that the Antichrist will not be Jewish or from one of the other monotheistic faiths.

The Antichrist and his false prophet will promote a system of their own and exalt it above all other forms of worship—both true and false (Dan. 11:36). He will feel the freedom to abolish and change religions as it suits his purposes (2 Thess. 2:4). The false prophet will "cause as many as [will] . . . not worship the image of the beast to be killed" (Rev. 13:15). While compelling the world to worship him, the Antichrist himself will worship Satan, the destroyer and bringer of death.

He will be particularly opposed to the worship of the true God (Dan. 11:36). God declares that such men are accursed, and the fate of the Antichrist bears this out.

The general course of his quest runs like this: the revived Roman Empire will become the strongest power in the world, and the Antichrist will become the ruler of this empire. He will set himself against God, and will persecute the Jewish people and those who refuse to receive "the mark of the beast" (Rev. 13). Jesus and His legions will defeat the Antichrist in the final battle of the war of Armageddon (Rev. 19:11–19). The Antichrist and the false prophet will be captured alive after this battle and thrown into the lake of fire (Rev. 19:20).

The Antichrist will not simply be handed the control of this revived Roman Empire (also called the Western Confederacy or fourth kingdom by some scholars)—he will have to seize the power. This Western Confederacy will initially be a confederation of ten kings. These ten kings will be in place and reigning before the advent of the Antichrist. When the Antichrist comes forward, he will meet and overcome initial opposition from three of the kings. He will then gain ascendancy over the remaining seven kings.

"After this I saw in the night visions, and behold, a fourth beast, dreadful and terrible, exceedingly strong. It had huge iron teeth; it was devouring, breaking in pieces, and trampling the residue with its feet. It was different from all the beasts that were before it, and it had ten horns. I was considering the horns, and there was another horn, a little one, coming up among them, before whom three of the first horns were plucked out by the roots. And there, in this horn, were eyes like the eyes of a man, and a mouth speaking pompous words. . . . The fourth beast shall be a fourth kingdom on earth, which shall be different from all other kingdoms, and shall devour the whole earth, trample it and break it in pieces. The ten horns are ten kings who shall arise from this kingdom. And another shall rise after them; he shall be different from the first ones, and shall subdue three kings. He shall speak pompous words against the Most High, shall persecute the saints of the Most High, and shall intend to change times and law. Then the saints shall be given into his hand for a time and times and half a time" (Dan. 7:7, 8, 23–25; cf. Rev. 13:1; 17:3, 7, 12, 16). Thus his rise to power will be all the more remarkable in that it will be accomplished without a large power base.

 ## 20. Is the Antichrist alive now?

He certainly could be, but we do not know for sure. The first event which will conclusively reveal the identity of the Antichrist is described in Daniel 9:26, 27: "And after the sixty-two weeks Messiah shall be cut off, but not for Himself; and the people of the prince who is to come shall destroy the city and the sanctuary. The end of it shall be with a flood, and till the end of the war desolations are determined. *Then he shall confirm a covenant with many for one week;* but in the middle of the week He shall bring an end to sacrifice and offering. And on the wing of abominations shall be one who makes desolate, even until the consummation, which is determined, is poured out on the desolate."

The person who signs the covenant with Israel guaranteeing her peace will be none other than the Antichrist. And the signing of the treaty launches the seven-year Tribulation.

 ## 21. Who is the false prophet?

He is the one described as the second beast of Revelation 13. He will be the religious leader who carries out the wishes of the first beast who is the Antichrist. In all likelihood, he will be Jewish, and will assist the Antichrist by performing miracles which will cause the world to worship him (Rev. 13:13–15)—miracles which include even giving "breath" to the image of the beast. The veneration of the Antichrist will be a tool that he uses to consolidate his political power. Once again, the false prophet will provide invaluable and infamous assistance in this area, administering the system whereby only those with "the mark of the beast" will be able to buy or sell (Rev. 13:2, 3, 14–17).

 ### 22. Is there really going to be a revived Roman Empire?

Yes, and it may already be in the making in the European Union. It shouldn't be forgotten that the Roman Empire, as vast as it was, was eventually split into Eastern and Western Empires, each with its own Caesar. Intriguingly, *both* capitals (Rome and Constantinople) are cities of seven hills, as the seat of the Antichrist's empire will be. And while we focus our attention on the European Union (EU), there is a common culture that unites peoples from Constantinople through to Afghanistan—a culture that is united by Islam and enmity toward the Jewish people.

I personally believe that the revived Roman Empire will grow out of the EU. The Bible specifies that this coming union will be comprised of at least 10 nations. I say *at least* because this may be a reference to 10 *leading* states, with other subordinate entities also belonging to the revived empire.

23. Is there going to be a one-world government?

Yes, it appears there will be. It seems to be in existence during the Tribulation and is described in Revelation 18. But the term "one-world government" may convey the wrong impression. It's not as if the Antichrist is going to rule over every single square foot of territory on earth. It is probably more accurate to say that the government headed by the Antichrist will be the one superpower in existence during the Tribulation.

The power of the Antichrist will be vast. He will be the head of what I believe will be the revived Roman Empire, consisting of *at least* ten nations. It will be *the* economic, military, and religious force on the planet. No nation or group of nations will be able to attempt much of anything apart from the blessing of this revived empire and succeed. Perhaps the greatest tribute to this is the fact that Israel will entrust its security to the Antichrist. She will not do this now with the U. S. A., but she will in the future with the Antichrist.

Yet we see throughout Tribulation that the Antichrist is involved in one military conflict after another. Most prominent among the other governments mentioned during the Tribulation are the king of the North (which I believe will be Russia), the kings of the East (which I believe will be China, India, and other Asiatic countries), and the kings of the South (which I believe will be a pan-Arab coalition).

For more on this, see page 121.

24. Is there going to be a one-world church?

Yes. There will be a one-world religion during the Great Tribulation. All who do not worship the Antichrist will not be able to survive. Revelation 17 describes this false religious system.

Even today, all around us we see the consolidation of Protestant religion through organizations like the National Council of Churches, the World Council of Churches, and the Consultation on Church Union. The leaders of these organizations, almost without exception, reject the cardinal doctrines of the faith.

But the important thing to note about the coming one-world religion is that it *won't* require every person on earth to believe the same things. It will be the embodiment of "tolerance," a religion of the least common denominator. As long as a religion or sect acknowledges the deity of the Antichrist, worships his image, and follows the leadership of the false prophet, the rest of what they believe will be tolerated.

For more on this, see page 121.

 ## 25. Who are the 144,000?

They are 144,000 servants from among the nation of Israel (Rev. 7:3–8). The Rapture and the initial events of the Tribulation will apparently be such that they will trust Christ and become saved. While the Antichrist makes a covenant with "many" Israelites (Dan. 9:27), by implication a few (at least 144,000) refuse to enter into this covenant. From each of the twelve tribes of Israel, at least 12,000 people will trust Christ (Rev. 7:5–8).

These 144,000 are the "firstfruits" (Rev. 14:4)—the forerunners of a multitude of Jews who will turn back to God at the second coming of Christ. They are "sealed" to identify them as servants of God and to protect them from the ravages of the Antichrist and the Tribulation. They are described as "ones who were not defiled with women" (Rev. 14:4). This may mean simply that they will be unmarried, that they will make a conscious decision to remain unmarried because of the rigors of the Tribulation, or it may be a figurative reference to the fact that they will keep themselves from all defiling relationships with the pagan world system.

For more on this, see pages 145–151.

 ## 26. Who are the two witnesses in Revelation 11?

They are not identified in Scripture. Some identify them as Moses and Elijah because of the types of miracles that they will perform, and because these two appeared with Christ on the mount of transfiguration (Matt. 17:1–8). Others identify the two witnesses as Enoch and Elijah. They reason that since Enoch and Elijah are the only two men who did not experience physical death, they will be brought back to earth so that they will experience it. The fact of the matter is that the identity of the two witnesses is not specified and probably cannot be known for sure. What is specified is the nature of their ministry and the signs that they will perform.

The two witnesses will prophesy for three-and-a-half years. Dressed in sackcloth, the garments of brokenness and repentance, they will call the inhabitants of the earth to repentance. They will enjoy supernatural protection and have the ability to stop the rain, turn waters into blood, and strike the earth with plagues. Killed by the Antichrist, these witnesses are dramatically and miraculously resurrected and will ascend into heaven while the entire world is watching.

 27. Will the weapons be as described in Ezekiel 38, and will horses be used in battles during the Tribulation?

They could very well be. Scripture does not say these will be the only types of warfare. Modern warfare was not in existence in Ezekiel's day, so he could very well have used the terminology of the warfare of his day to describe future battles. On the other hand, don't forget that the Tribulation will be a time of unprecedented disruption, destruction, and mayhem. What if the high-tech weapons in the arsenals of the world are used up, or destroyed? What if nations can no longer secure the fuel to power them? What if the technicians and specialists who operate them are dead? Nations will still find a way to wage war with one another. If they can't use missiles, they'll use sharp sticks. If they can't use tanks, then maybe they'll use horses.

On the other hand, I don't think in order to adhere to a literal interpretation we must say actual horses will be used. Literal interpretation doesn't demand that Jesus be an actual door just because He says, "I am the door." But literal interpretation does demand that Jesus *is* what a door *does*—which is include and exclude. So from Ezekiel 38 we know that there will be a conflict that will leave destruction in its wake.

28. Who is the power from the North in Ezekiel 38?

In the Bible, Palestine is central. Every direction given is in relation to it. It is generally believed by the majority of prophetic students that this power will be Russia and her satellite nations.

Virtually all of the locations mentioned in this passage are located in modern-day Turkey, Syria, Iraq, and Iran. While older scholarship identified the locations as being within the borders of Russia, we now know that this isn't the case. Nevertheless, this only leads me to believe that Russia will extend its empire into these countries by the time the prophecy of Ezekiel 38 comes to pass.

29. Who are the armies from the East who will invade Israel?

These are the armies from the Asiatic peoples who will cross the supernaturally-prepared Euphrates to seek to conquer Israel, the center of the government of the Antichrist. Once again, their identity isn't specified beyond this, except that it refers to the kings (plural) of the East—so clearly more than one country or power block from the East will be involved. When we here in the West think about people in the east, we naturally think about China and Japan. And I believe that they will be among the kings of the East, but don't forget about India, Afghanistan, Korea, Vietnam, or that the most populous *Muslim* country in the world is Indonesia.

 ## 30. Who is the king from the South who will invade Israel?

This is a reference to a pan-Arabic block of nations from modern-day Libya, Egypt, Sudan, and Ethiopia. It seems likely that Russia will incite these nations to come up against Israel and then intervene before the Arabs conquer the land. There is strong Muslim influence in these countries, and with that comes a hatred for Israel and a passion to see their holy sites in Jerusalem under complete Arab control. It probably won't take much prodding on Russia's part to spur these nations to action.

 ## 31. What is the battle of Armageddon?

This is the last world war. It will be the final conflict in a series of battles between world powers over the city of Jerusalem and the land of Palestine. It is therefore more of a campaign that rages through most of the last half of the Tribulation than one single battle.

Armageddon itself is a vast plain in the nation of Israel. It is there that the kings of North, South, and East will assemble to contend with the Antichrist and lay claim to Jerusalem and the land of Israel. This puts these vast alliances in conflict with one another.

Somehow, once they are gathered, they manage to put their differences aside and join forces to oppose God

Himself. It is to the valley of Armageddon that the Lord Jesus descends along with "the armies which are in heaven" (Rev. 19:14) to defeat the armies of the earth along with Satan, the Antichrist, and the false prophet. Jesus will then reign over the earth as King of kings and Lord of lords.

For more on this, see pages 89, 95.

32. When will the Tribulation saints be raised?

They will be raised sometime during the 75-day gap between the end of the Tribulation and the beginning of the Millennium. Revelation 20:4–6 refers to a resurrection before the Millennium and one after it: "And I saw thrones, and they sat on them, and judgment was committed to them. Then I saw the souls of those who had been beheaded for their witness to Jesus and for the word of God, who had not worshiped the beast or his image, and had not received his mark on their foreheads or on their hands. And they lived and reigned with Christ for a thousand years. But the rest of the dead did not live again until the thousand years were finished. This is the first resurrection. Blessed and holy is he who has part in the first resurrection. Over such the second death has no power, but they shall be priests of God and of Christ, and shall reign with Him a thousand years."

In the resurrection before the Millennium, Old Testament saints and Tribulation saints will be raised. In the resurrection after the Millennium all the unsaved of all ages will be raised to appear at the Great White Throne Judgment.

33. Will Old Testament saints be raptured at the same time church saints are?

No. The "dead in Christ" are the ones who rise to meet the Lord in the air at the Rapture. Old Testament saints are not described as those "in Christ." At the Rapture only the "dead in Christ" will be resurrected and then "caught up" to be with the Lord.

Daniel 12:11, 12 describes a 75-day gap between the end of the Tribulation and the beginning of the Millennium. During this time, Old Testament saints will be resurrected, and will rule with Christ during the Millennium. The Scriptures do not say when or if Old Testament saints are judged, and we must respect that silence.

For more on this, see pages 88, 89.

 ## 34. How is it that "all Israel shall be saved"?

The Jewish people will undergo fierce persecution at the hands of the Antichrist, and many will be killed. But many will also be saved. In fact, as I mentioned earlier, more people will come to faith in Christ during the Tribulation than during any other seven-year period in human history. Undoubtedly the 144,000 "Jewish evangelists" that God commissions at the beginning of the Tribulation will play a role in this—but they will not be the only instrument God uses.

At the end of the Tribulation, the Jewish people will pass under the rod of God's judgment. Many will be condemned and killed. Those who pass this judgment will be those who have trusted Jesus as their Messiah. They will be given a new heart, and having trusted Jesus as their

Messiah, they will enter the Millennium alive to repopulate Israel.

So "all Israel will be saved" in the sense that the only
ones remaining after God's judgment at the end of the
Tribulation will be those who are saved.

 ## 35. Is there a future Millennium?

Yes. The Millennium will be a thousand-year period
in which Christ will set up a kingdom and rule over the
entire earth (Rev. 20:4). It will begin about seventy-five
days after the end of the Tribulation (Dan. 12:12). This
thousand-year period is explicitly mentioned *six* times in
six verses (Rev. 20:2–7).

The Millennium will serve at least two useful purposes in the program of God. One will be to fulfill His
promises—especially the promises that He made to Abraham (in Gen. 12:2, 3). There are four central features to
this promise of God.

The *first* feature is that He would make a great nation
of Abraham's progeny. The *second* feature is related to the
first, and it is the promise to Abraham of a multitude of descendants (Gen. 15:5). To be sure, this promise has been
fulfilled in part, since Abraham does have a multitude of
descendants through his sons Ishmael and Isaac. But in the
Millennium, he will have even more because people will
be healthier and live longer (Isa. 35:6, 7; 65:20, 22, 23).

The *third* feature is that Israel will be given "everlasting possession" of the promised land, the boundaries of
which are set forth in Genesis 15:18–21. The nation of Israel has yet to control this entire section of land.

The *fourth* feature is that the entire world would be blessed through Abraham. This was fulfilled through Jesus Christ and will be fulfilled when He rules on the earth during the Millennium, bringing both spiritual *and* material blessing to mankind.

In the Millennium God also will fulfill the promises He made to the nation of Israel. One notable promise to Israel is found in Deuteronomy 30:1–9 (scholars call it the Palestinian Covenant). Because God has bound Himself to do certain things in this covenant, there must be a time for God to do them—and this time will be the Millennium.

In the Millennium God will fulfill some promises He made to King David. God promised David that "your house and your kingdom shall be established forever before you. Your throne shall be established forever" (2 Sam. 7:16). This literal kingdom promised to David will come to pass in the Millennium when Christ, the Son of David according to the flesh (Matt. 1:1; Isa. 11:1, 2), will rule upon the earth. Not only will Christ rule in the Millennium, David will assist Him by ruling over Israel. That is, Christ will rule indirectly over Israel through David, who will serve as Christ's regent.

Jerusalem will be the center of the earth during the Millennium because Christ will rule from there (cf. Isa. 33:17). Jesus will rule through a hierarchy that will consist of David (Ezek. 37:24, 25), resurrected believers (Rev. 20:4), and those Jews who enter the millennial kingdom (Matt. 25:14–30).

The Father and the Son will have a direct teaching ministry during the Millennium, and they will raise up other competent teachers as well (Isa. 54:13; Mic. 4:2; Jer.

3:15; Isa. 60:1–3). This will result in the knowledge of the glory of the Lord and the ability to worship Him in purity (Zeph. 3:9).

The sun (and consequently the moon) will shine more brightly in the Millennium, and this will no doubt be one of the factors responsible for the overall prosperity of the period (Isa. 30:26; Mal. 4:2). Yet in spite of this, the splendor of the glory of the Lord will far outshine the sun (Isa. 24:23).

The Millennium will be a time of great prosperity and activity (Joel 2:24–26; Amos 9:13, 14; Isa. 32:17, 18; 65:21, 22).

The violent, predatory nature of the animal world will cease in the Millennium (Isa. 11:6–9; Hos. 2:18; Zech. 10:7, 8).

For more on this, see pages 81–98, 113, 114.

 ## 36. Who will enter the future Millennium?

Only those who are rightly related to Christ the King will enter the Millennium. The pioneers of the Millennium will be those who trusted Christ and survived the Tribulation, whether Jew or Gentile. They are the ones who will repopulate the earth and live under the government of the Lord Jesus.

Resurrected saints, both from before the Day of Pentecost and after, will rule on the earth with Jesus. The Scripture doesn't specify in what way we will rule with Jesus, but it does affirm that we will. Some speculate the New Jerusalem will be hovering over the earth in those days, and that it will be the abode of the saints, and the place from which they can freely travel both to earth and heaven.

For more on this, see pages 81–98.

 ## 37. Will there be births and deaths in the Millennium?

Isaiah 65:20–23 seems to indicate that there will be: "No more shall an infant from there live but a few days, nor an old man who has not fulfilled his days; for the child shall die one hundred years old, but the sinner being one hundred years old shall be accursed. They shall build houses and inhabit them; they shall plant vineyards and eat their fruit. They shall not build and another inhabit; they shall not plant and another eat; for as the days of a tree, so shall be the days of My people, and My elect shall long enjoy the work of their hands. They shall not labor in vain, nor bring forth children for trouble; for they shall be the descendants of the blessed of the Lord, and their offspring with them."

According to this passage, the sorrow in bearing children will be taken away during the Millennium, and a life span of but 100 years will be viewed as a tragedy.

 ## 38. How will Christ reign forever since the Millennium is only 1,000 years long?

After the Millennium, the final rebellion of Satan, the destruction of the present heavens and earth, and the Great White Throne Judgment, God will create a new heaven and a new earth, and upon this new earth the celestial city of New Jerusalem will descend. This period, which begins with the creation of the new heavens and earth, is called by scholars the eternal state.

Abraham obeyed God because "he waited for the city [i.e., the New Jerusalem] which has foundations, whose builder and maker is God" (Heb. 11:10). In fact, the New Jerusalem has been prepared exactly for people like Abel, Enoch, Noah, Abraham, and Sarah (Heb. 11:16). The inhabitants of the New Jerusalem are enumerated in Hebrews 12:22–24:

- an innumerable company of angels
- the general assembly and church of the firstborn who are registered in heaven—the church, firstborn because of their union with Christ
- God, the Judge of all
- the spirits of just men made perfect—those who came to believe in the times of the Old Testament, the Tribulation, or the Millennium
- Jesus, the Mediator of the New Covenant

The inhabitants will all have glorified bodies because "flesh and blood cannot inherit the kingdom of God; nor does corruption inherit incorruption" (1 Cor. 15:50). But this raises the question, "Why is the tree of life in the New Jerusalem described as being there for 'the healing of the nations' if the only inhabitants of the city have immortal and incorruptible bodies?" The answer to this question is that the word translated "healing" carries with it the idea of serving or ministering. Thus the tree of life will enhance the enjoyment of life in the New Jerusalem—not heal illnesses which don't even exist.

John describes the city in Revelation 21:1—22:5.

Among the many notable aspects of the city is that it "had no need of the sun or of the moon to shine in it, for the glory of God illuminated it, and the Lamb is its light" (Rev. 21:23; cf. 22:5). This is also predicted in Isaiah 60:19, 20:

> The sun shall no longer be your light by day,
> Nor for brightness shall the moon give light to you;
> But the LORD will be to you an everlasting light,
> And your God your glory.
> Your sun shall no longer go down,
> Nor shall your moon withdraw itself;
> For the LORD will be your everlasting light,
> And the days of your mourning shall be ended.

So in other words, Scripture indicates Christ will go on reigning forever after the brief Satanic rebellion, for then the kingdoms of this world become the kingdom of our Lord and of His Christ, and He shall reign forever (Rev. 11:15).

 ### 39. What will heaven be like?

The thing that will make heaven heavenly is that we will be with the Lord Jesus. In heaven we will have new bodies, and not only will the old sinful nature be gone, but the curse and the effects which are now all around us will be fully and finally gone. Because of that, we will experience no more sorrow, sin, pain or death. But not only will we not experience them, we won't cause others to experience them either. We will be living the life that was intended for us, with the Savior who loves us, worshiping Him and joyfully giving thanks to Him for all that He has done in that beautiful place with streets of gold.

For more on this, see pages 72, 73.

40. Are the streets of heaven made of real gold?

They may not actually be gold, since gold tarnishes and decays. But on the other hand, since tarnishing and decay have to do with the curse, and since the effects of the curse are removed in heaven, they may very well be gold.

Regardless of whether the streets are made of what we today consider "gold," they will, like gold, be comprised of the most costly and enduring metal.

This same question could be asked about jewels that make up the New Jerusalem and so many other details that are revealed to us about heaven. There is an old saying, but a good one: If the plain sense makes common sense, seek no other sense. The New Jerusalem may very well be constructed of stones like the jasper, sapphire, emerald, etc. that we know today. If they are not the same, they will look the same and be magnificent to behold.

 ## 41. Will we know each other in heaven?

There is every reason to believe that we will know each other. One of the many joys of heaven, I suspect, will be joyous reunions with family and friends. I don't know what we'll look like. I don't know that we'll look the same as we do now, but we will be recognizable. I suspect we'll all look around a certain median age with no age or sex differences.

But I wonder if behind this question is a certain lack of understanding about how amazing the fellowship in heaven is going to be. We will be with the Lord Jesus. The

"God-shaped" vacuum inside of all of us will be filled, and we'll feel more complete and fulfilled than ever before. Not only that, but the fellowship that we'll enjoy with the saints in heaven will be way beyond the richest experience of fellowship we've had on earth. So even if we won't be able to recognize others in heaven, it will take nothing away from the experience.

 ### 42. Are the crowns we receive as rewards literal or symbolic, and what will believers do with them in heaven?

I believe that they will be literal. We have to have something which belongs to us in order to be able to cast them at the feet of Jesus, as the Scripture declares we will do. It's very important to also note here that there is nothing we do to *merit* these crowns; instead the Father in His mercy rewards us with crowns for faithful service. By "faithful service" I mean deeds done while here on earth for His cause—not our own. Deeds done for our own cause will result in the *loss* of reward.

The Scripture doesn't address whether the deeds we have done on earth will have any significance after we have cast our crowns at His feet. There are ranks among the angels, and differences of responsibility while ruling during the Millennium, so we might have ranks or stations during the Eternal State—the Scripture just doesn't say. However, we do know that *if* there are ranks or stations in the Eternal State, they will cause neither pride nor jealousy, since those things have to do with the old nature.

43. Who are the twenty-four elders?

They are twenty-four human beings who have been given glorified bodies and who surround the magnificent throne of God in heaven. They are not identified beyond this in Scripture, although several suggestions have been offered:

- Some like me believe that they are drawn from the ranks of church-age saints.
- Others believe that twelve of the elders, one each from the twelve tribes of Israel, and twelve drawn from the ranks of the church—perhaps even the apostles.
- Still others believe that they are drawn from the ranks of the angels.

I believe that the first position is the most likely. The middle position seems less likely to me since God has separate programs for the church and Israel. The third position seems the least likely, since the Greek word for "elder" is used nowhere else with reference to an angel.

For more on this, see pages 145–151.

 44. What happens to Christians at death?

They go immediately into the presence of the Lord where they will be forever. They will receive a glorified body at the time of the future resurrection.

This raises the question of whether we will have some sort of intermediate body for the period between when we die and when we are given new bodies. I tend to believe that the answer to this question is "yes." But the

Scriptures simply do not address this issue. Yet the most important issue is not what form we're in during this intermediate time—but who we are with. And during this time between death and resurrection, whatever our form, we will be in the glorious, comforting presence of the Lord.

At the Rapture, whether we are living on the earth or have just experienced resurrection at the instant of God's trumpet call, we will be given new bodies. The new bodies will be related to our old bodies in the same sense that a corn stalk issues forth from a corn seed. Our resurrection bodies will be free from sin, sickness, or death, and be like Jesus' body after His resurrection.

For more on this, see pages 64, 65.

45. What is the Judgment Seat of Christ?

The Greek word used refers to an elevated stand used for the judge of a sporting activity, both to observe the contestants and give awards to the contestants. So, like contestants, we will appear before Jesus, who will evaluate our lives, and as a result reward will be either lost or gained.

The eternal destiny of those who appear before Christ is not at issue, but we will give an account of our lives, be recompensed for deeds done in the body—whether good or bad—and receive reward or experience the loss of reward. Jesus will examine our fruit, and simply having leaves won't be enough. It seems that our works will be evaluated more on quality than on quantity—did we do them for His glory, or our own?

And though our eternal destiny is not at issue, the prospect of appearing before this seat causes a purifying terror or fear of the Lord.

For more on this, see pages 66, 89.

 ## 46. What happens to non-Christians at death?

Their spirits go to a temporary place of punishment known by the Greek word, *Hades.* As we see from the parable of the rich man and Lazarus in Luke 16:19–31, Hades is a place of "torment," "agony," and "flame." The suffering is so great in this place that even a single drop of water on the tongue would provide relief.

Non-Christians are kept in Hades until the resurrection at the end of the Millennium. After their resurrection, they will appear at the Great White Throne Judgment before the Lord Jesus. He was the one who offered them another way by dying on the cross in their place and for their sins. But these people would have none of it, and so they now experience Jesus as judge.

In the presence of Jesus, "books were opened. And another book was opened, which is the Book of Life. And the dead were judged according to their works, by the things which were written in the books" (Rev. 20:12). These people, judged on the basis of whether their works can satisfy the offended righteousness of a holy God, will be found wanting, and they will be condemned to the lake of fire, there to experience torment forever and ever.

For more on this, see page 89.

47. What is the Great White Throne Judgment?

It is the final dread judgment. All the unsaved of all ages will appear at this Judgment. It is described in Revelation 20:11–15. Jesus sits upon this throne. And His aspect is fearsome—so much so that heaven and earth flee from His presence. And with good reason, for all who appear before this throne will be condemned to spend eternity in conscious suffering in the lake of fire.

As each person appears before the Lord Jesus, a series of books is reviewed in which their deeds have been recorded. One book in particular stands out—it is the book of life. Because there is none righteous, no not one, every person who stands before Christ will find that their works are inadequate and—having failed to trust Him— their names will not be found in the book of life.

For more on this, see pages 65, 75, 89, 100, 101, 116, 166.

48. Will the unsaved suffer eternally?

Yes. They will suffer in what the Bible calls "the lake of fire." Conscious, eternal torment awaits those who have not trusted Christ as their Savior. He Himself said those not rightly related to Him would "go away into eternal punishment" (Matt. 25:46).

I believe that whatever heaven is, hell is the opposite. Those who are ushered into heaven will dwell there forever. Conversely, those who are consigned to the lake of fire will be there forever. There are degrees of reward for those who dwell in heaven, and I believe there will be degrees of punishment for those in hell. I believe that Jesus lends credence to this as he sums up the parable of the faithful steward: "And that servant who knew his master's will, and did not prepare himself or do according to his will, shall be beaten with many stripes. But he who did not know, yet committed things deserving of stripes, shall be beaten with few. For everyone to whom much is given, from him much will be required; and to whom much has been committed, of him they will ask the more" (Luke 12:47, 48). Thus some person in a remote location who never heard the gospel would be consigned to the lake of fire, but that person's punishment would not be as severe as, say, an Adolf Hitler.

For more on this, see pages 74, 75.

 ### 49. Are the flames in hell literal?

The punishment is real and is felt. If the flames are not literal, the result of being engulfed in them will be worse than physical fire. But once again, if the plain sense makes literal sense, seek no other sense. There is no reason not to understand the flames of hell to be literal, and in every passage that describes hell or punishment in the afterlife, flame is used to describe it. So the flames are probably literal, and the torment of those in hell is *definitely* literal.

For more on this, see pages 73–74, 77.

 ### 50. How can hell be outer darkness if there is eternal fire?

The Bible says both things are true. Some people also question how hell can be a lake (associated with water, which extinguishes flame) of fire. But even here on earth, most of us will remember images from the Gulf War of pools of crude oil boiling with flame. Some liquids burn quite intensely, and in the case of hell, eternally so.

The "fire" of hell may not dispense light but it will be just as painful. And that is the important thing to remember. Whatever it is, hell is a place to be avoided at all cost. No sacrifice on our part is too great or small to spread the everlasting gospel. Hell *is* real—and we need to be on a dead run to depopulate it.

For more on this, see pages 68, 74.

As the angel thundered, "The testimony of Jesus is the spirit of prophecy" (Rev. 19:10). In the pages that follow, you will be given a background which will greatly increase your understanding and appreciation of Bible prophecy. Even so, come quickly, Lord Jesus!

Part 1

THE ISSUES

1

Another Book on Prophecy?

Why another book about the future? That seems to be a fair question since the market has been flooded with material on prophecy in recent years. No new view of things to come will be set forth in these pages. Rather, I will compare and contrast the various eschatologies that already exist among evangelicals. This is the primary reason for this volume. Its message is surely urgent and needs desperately to be heeded.

Evangelicals and Fundamentalists

A word of orientation and background will help us. Just as there are liberals and conservatives in the political world, similar segments exist in the religious world. There are also variations, of course, within these two groupings, both in politics and religion. For example, there are extreme liberals and moderate liberals, just as there are strong conservatives and moderate conservatives. Other descriptions abound also, such as right- and left-wing.

It often happens that the label one is given or the position one is said to embrace is a rather subjective thing.

We often set ourselves up as the standard of judgment. Too many times we define our own view as the center, the true one, and then assign others accordingly—left or right of us.

In 1909 two Christian laymen made possible the publication of a twelve-volume set called, *The Fundamentals*.[1] Three million copies of this scholarly defense of the faith were circulated. This monumental work restated and clearly defined biblical, historic Christianity. The contributors were men of great faith and scholarship. The work was a defense of the faith against the attacks that had been and were being made upon it by secular philosophy, unbelieving science, and especially modern, liberal theology.

Five major doctrines and themes related to them were set forth in the twelve small volumes. The major doctrines were:

1. the inspiration and authority of Scripture,
2. the virgin birth of Christ,
3. the deity of Christ,
4. the substitutionary atonement of Christ, and
5. the bodily resurrection of Christ and His second coming.

A quick look at the list tells us that the two doctrines around which all the discussion revolved were the person and work of Christ and the inspiration of the Bible.

On the basis of these fundamentals, the evangelicals (or the fundamentalists as they became known) and the liberals (or modernists as they were called then) were separated. The lines were clearly drawn. Those who embraced and defended these traditional doctrines of the faith were called fundamentalists and those who did not were called modernists.

Today other terms are sometimes used to designate these two groups. Modernists are now called liberals and fundamentalists are sometimes called evangelicals. Actually the word *evangelical* is a biblical one and when used in its historic sense, describes those who believe with conviction the five fundamentals of the faith in addition to other cardinal doctrines.[2]

As is the case with most words, *evangelical* and *evangelicalism* have been given new meanings and need to be explained, but so do the words *fundamental* and *fundamentalism.* They too are sometimes used today to represent more than belief in the five fundamentals of the faith. Descriptive words like these all have overtones or connotations that are undesirable to some who are otherwise content with the designation.

When used in this volume the term *evangelical* refers to one who accepts the great cardinal doctrines of the faith. Some who do so are, of course, more vociferous in their defense of those fundamentals than others. Because of this, there are differences regarding associations which Christians have with each other, depending on how important those differences are perceived to be. The term *evangelical,* however, designates one who is orthodox in his beliefs, in contrast to one who is unorthodox.

This study will deal with only one of the five fundamentals presented above. While all who are legitimately called evangelical or fundamental believe all five, and more besides, there are considerable differences in the ranks over how to understand some of the details concerning the second coming of Christ.

He will return! Evangelicals agree fully on that. On

the question of what specifics will be associated with His
return and what the exact order of events will be, and the
sequence of time in which they will come to pass, however, there is very little agreement.

The Historical Setting

Many Christians consider all the fuss about the future
unnecessary. They view the discussion of any order of
end-time events as inconsequential and a big waste of
time and effort. As far as they are concerned, it is more important that we spread the gospel than it is to debate what
they consider to be trivialities about how events will unfold in the future.

On the other hand, theologians and many Christian
leaders hold tenaciously to particular views of future happenings. Denominations, mission agencies, schools, para-
church ministries and other Christian organizations, as
well as individuals, are divided over God's plan for the future. Much time and effort is spent in defense of the various views. Why? Prophecy is in the proverbial ring all
right, to draw from the sport of boxing. I doubt very much
that many would deny that. But the question remains,
Why? We are going to try to find out why in this study.

Viewed from the perspective of a casual onlooker,
the evangelical world is splintered over the order of things
to come. The Body of Christ is truly fractured over future
events. What is more, the divisions have existed for a long
time. Since the third century of the Christian era, the controversy has raged. It has always been serious, but in the
last twenty or twenty-five years the conflict has increased
to the point of crisis.

A notable theologian with special interest in the subject of prophecy and future events made this observation
regarding the renewed interest in the question of future
events:

> The events of the last quarter of a century or more have
> had tremendous impact on the thinking of the scholarly
> world. In philosophy there has been a trend toward real-
> ism and increasing interest in ultimate values and ethics.
> In science, the moral significance of scientific knowl-
> edge and the growing realization that physical science is
> a part of world life and meaning have emerged. In theol-
> ogy there has been what amounts to a similar revolution,
> particularly in the study of prophecy.[3]

There are three major belief systems regarding God's
program for the future. Equally dedicated, sincere, and
godly men have contended for these. *Premillennialism* is
the view that Christ will return and institute a kingdom of
perfect peace and righteousness on earth that will last for
one thousand years. After this reign of true peace, eternity
begins. *Amillennialism* is the view that when Christ returns, eternity begins with no prior thousand-year (millennial) reign on earth. The *postmillennial* view (though out
of favor for some time, is again gaining popularity) has it
that through the church's influence the world will be
Christianized before Christ returns. Immediately following
His return, eternity begins. Each of these views will be explained further in Chapters 3—5.

Whatever else may be said of these views, one thing
is sure: They cannot all be right. The views cancel out
each other. I suspect that a good number of Christians
would not be disappointed if all three systems were can-

celled out and the tug-of-war among believers over prophecy would cease. No doubt many would like to call for a moratorium on the prophecy debate. For them, that would indeed be the coming of kingdom bliss.

Regrettably, the prophecy war probably will not stop. But a better understanding of the reasons for the conflict will surely lessen the tension. The differences will probably prevail until the Lord Himself comes and fulfills His Word. So let us not engage in wishful thinking. We must face the facts and evaluate the situation as it is. The time has come for us to take a long, careful look at the various views and their relation to God's Word. It is also essential that we see the importance of unfulfilled prophecy and its relationship to other areas of the Bible's teaching. Last-days views, like all other theological issues, are never held in isolation.

Wrongly, the three views of the future defined above have often been set forth as primarily the result of one's interpretation of the references to the "thousand years" in Revelation 20:1–7. This is far too simplistic an answer. Instead of one's interpretation of this phrase determining his millennial view, it is really the other way around. One's millennial system arrived at on other biblical grounds determines how Revelation 20:1–7 will be interpreted.

Scriptural teaching of the Millennium or kingdom is by no means confined to specific kingdom terminology. One who could not be classified as a particular friend of evangelicalism made this point with real force:

> For the concept of the Kingdom of God involves in a real
> sense the total message of the Bible. Not only does it
> loom large in the teaching, it is to be found in one form

or another through the length and breadth of the Bible. . . . Old Testament and New Testament thus stand together as the two acts of a single drama. Act 1 points to its conclusion in Act 2 and without it the play is an incomplete unsatisfying thing. But Act 2 must be read in light of Act 1 else its meaning would be missed. Where the play is organically one, the Bible is one book. Had we to give that book a title, we might with justice call it, "The Book of the Coming Kingdom of God."[4]

A Call to Consider

It is hoped that this book will contribute to the reduction of the warfare among evangelicals over the understanding of unfulfilled prophecies. I have not written to stir up more controversy or to enlarge the battle over end-time events. I am convinced there is a good deal of misunderstanding and misrepresentation in the furor over the future. No doubt much of this is because of insufficient information or misdirected zeal, and maybe some of each. This book is intended to help meet this need.

What is said here will surely not solve all the problems, eliminate all the differences, and bring about a cessation of the war over end-time events among evangelicals. The book is designed, however, to provide evangelicals with a better understanding of their own views and why Christians differ over these matters. With this understanding I hope there will also come a deeper commitment to the Lord Jesus Christ, the living Word of God, and the Bible, the written Word of God. When this occurs, there will be a deeper love for the people of God regardless of their understanding of things to come.

Several positive reasons, therefore, prompt me to write another book on prophecy. First, I want to set forth the various views held by evangelicals with regard to the future. Second, the reasons for their differences need to be explored and explained. Third, I want to alert the Christian public concerning the intensity of the battle over the Bible's teaching about events to come and offer a suggested solution. Most clergymen and church leaders are well aware of the conflict, but many laypeople need more information. They have a right to know why the people of God, who agree on all the essentials or fundamentals of the faith, differ so widely and battle so tenaciously over prophecy. Why fight over future events anyway? What makes this doctrine so different from the others over which Christians disagree? These are basic questions of this study.

Fourth, I want to suggest that evangelicals begin to practice in their use of prophecy what they preach in their doctrine of the family of God. It is time that we start behaving like brothers and sisters in the heavenly family. Each child in the household of faith is needed, and we must never forget that the exercise of Christian love is just as essential in eschatology as it is in every other area of God's truth and Christian living.

If what I have said in these pages makes even the smallest contribution toward easing the tensions over events to come, it will have been well worth the effort.

For Further Thought

1. Why do you think there is so much interest in prophecy lately?

2. How can it be determined which doctrines are essential to the faith and which ones are not?

3. Do you think there are any differences between those who wish to be called fundamentalists and those who prefer the name evangelical? If so, what are some of those differences?

4. Think about some of the Christian organizations you are familiar with and try to verbalize their official view of eschatology.

5. If I succeed in accomplishing my goals in writing this book, how will it help you?

 Digging Deeper

The original twelve-volume set of *The Fundamentals* first published in 1909 consisted of articles contributed by recognized biblical scholars such as Benjamin B. Warfield, Melvin Grove Kyle, and H. C. G. Moule. The authors came from a wide spectrum of background and expertise—Episcopal bishops, attorneys, theologians, and Egyptologists. Almost all the articles defended the inspiration and authority of the Bible and some aspect of the person and work of Christ. Of the ninety articles included in the twelve small volumes, only one dealt specifically with the return of Christ to the earth. In that article entitled, "The Coming of Christ," Charles R. Erdman of Princeton Theological Seminary argued that the return of Christ was indeed a fundamental of the historic Christian faith. In his defense of this cardinal doctrine Erdman insisted Christ's return would be personal and glorious. He was quick to point out the fallacies of the liberal or modernistic view.

Christ's promised coming again, he argued, was not to be confused with His spiritual presence with believers, the coming of the Holy Spirit on Pentecost, providential events of history, or the believer's death.

Interestingly, in the article Erdman, an amillennialist, did not belabor his differences with opposing premillennial and postmillennial views. Rather, his guns were leveled at the theological liberals of his day and their rejection of the Bible as God's infallible Word.

For those who wish to examine firsthand the basic content of these volumes as well as the manner in which the conflict was waged, see the two-volume presentation of the original twelve volumes by Charles Feinberg (Grand Rapids: Kregel, 1958).

Others may want to dig deeper into the present state of affairs in the evangelical/fundamentalist discussions. For this see "History and Development" in my *Neo-Evangelicalism*. Also see Edward Dobson's *In Search of Unity* and Ernest Pickering's response in "Should Fundamentalists and Evangelicals Seek Closer Ties?" in the *Baptist Bulletin*, March 1986, 9–38.

2

Evangelical Agreement on Things to Come

From Genesis to Revelation, the Bible is filled with prophecy. It has been said that one-fourth of the books of the Bible are prophetic in nature and one-fifth of the actual text of Scripture was prophetic when it was written.[1] Whether or not these percentages are altogether accurate is debatable. However, it must be admitted that Scripture abounds with prophecy and that much of what has been predicted has already come to pass.[2]

Perhaps the best examples of fulfilled prophecies are those related to the Lord Jesus Christ. More than three hundred prophecies were fulfilled at the first advent of Christ. An example of some of these related to His earthly ministry and sacrificial death are included in the following charts, Christ's Ministry Predicted and Christ's Death Predicted.[3]

There are, to be sure, a significant number of predictions made in the Bible that have not yet come to pass. These are the chief concern of this book regardless of which view one takes of the order of future events or the manner in which they are to be fulfilled. All who accept

Christ's Ministry Predicted

Element of Christ's Ministry	Old Testament Prediction	New Testament Fulfillment
Location	Isaiah 9:1, 2	Matthew 4:13–16
Power	Isaiah 11:2	Luke 3:22; 4:1
Saving Character	Isaiah 61:1	Luke 4:16–19
Healing Character	Isaiah 53:4	Matthew 8:16–17
Miracles	Isaiah 35:5–6	Matthew 11:4–5
Inclusion of Gentiles	Isaiah 42:1, 6	Luke 2:32
Zeal	Psalm 69:9	John 2:17
Serving Character	Isaiah 42:1–4	Matthew 12:15–21
Humility	Zechariah 9:9	Matthew 21:4–5
Rejection	Isaiah 53:3	John 1:11

Christ's Death Predicted

Event of the Passion	Old Testament Prediction	New Testament Fulfillment
To be deserted	Zechariah 13:7	Matthew 26:31
To be scourged and spat on	Isaiah 50:6	Matthew 26:67
To be given vinegar to drink	Psalm 69:21	Matthew 27:34, 48
To be pierced with nails	Psalm 22:16	Luke 23:33
To be forsaken by God	Psalm 22:1	Matthew 27:46
To be surrounded by enemies	Isaiah 22:7–8	Matthew 27:39–40
To be numbered with transgressors	Isaiah 53:12	Mark 15:27–28
To agonize with thirst	Psalm 22:15	John 19:28
To commend His spirit to God	Psalm 31:5	Luke 23:46
To have His garments distributed	Psalm 22:18	John 19:23–24
To have no bone broken	Psalm 34:20	John 19:33–36
To be buried with the rich	Isaiah 53:9	Matthew 27:57–60
To rise from the dead	Psalm 16:9–10	Acts 2:27, 31
To ascend into glory	Psalm 68:18	Ephesians 4:8

Chart 4

the Bible as God's infallible Word agree; they have not yet been fulfilled but will be in the future.

The order in which the major unfulfilled prophecies are presented is not significant. No particular emphasis is intended by the presentation and it is not my purpose to defend any particular scheme of prophecy by the order. Evangelicals agree there is unfulfilled prophecy and that is what needs to be emphasized here. Those who love the Lord and His Word have little argument with each other about the certainty of these future events. What they do argue about though (and sometimes in very unchristian ways) is the *order* in which these things will be fulfilled, the time sequence. Indeed, orthodox Christians argue vociferously over events to come and do not hesitate to part company because of differences over end-time events.

Our primary concern, in this chapter, will not be over areas of difference, but with those prophecies of Scripture that all evangelicals agree have not yet been fulfilled. In other words, we first want to know what the major unfulfilled prophecies are—the events still to come—that evangelicals do not fight over. What prophecies are accepted by most evangelicals?

The Immortality of the Soul

Belief in the immortality of the soul implies an eternal state of some kind. (More will be said about the eternal state later in this chapter.) "Immortality means the eternal, continuous, conscious existence of the soul after the death of the body."[4] Strictly speaking, this doctrine does not by itself demand that there be a resurrected body. Evangelicals do believe, however, that there will be the resurrection of the body. (There will be more on this later also.) Evangelicals concur that both Old and New Testaments teach clearly the immortality of man's soul. Without doubt, the resurrection of Christ is positive proof of life beyond the grave.

The Intermediate State

"By the intermediate state is meant that realm or condition in which souls exist between death and the resurrection."[5] Evangelicals do differ over the nature of the believer's existence in the intermediate state, but there is a general consensus that there is such a state. They believe the intermediate state for the believer is a time of conscious existence, a state of rest and happiness and freedom from sin and pain, in the very presence of Christ. For the unbeliever it is a state of temporary suffering to be followed by the judgment and eternal separation from God in the lake of fire.

The Future Bodily Resurrection

From the beginning of the Christian era, belief in future divine judgment was generally associated with belief in the certainty of the future resurrection of all people; the dead will be raised so that they might be judged. The Apostles' Creed, the earliest apostolic testimony about Christ, refers to the Judgment when it states that, "Christ shall come to judge the quick [living] and the dead," but not everyone agreed that that statement meant there would be a resurrection.

When Jesus was on earth, some believed in the future resurrection of all people while others did not. The

Pharisees accepted the doctrine but the Sadducees rejected it (Matt. 22:23; Acts 23:8). Their differences over the resurrection did not, of course, keep them from joining together in their opposition to the Savior. They were perfectly willing to overlook their otherwise rigidly held views so they could form a united front against Christ.

When Paul preached the doctrine of the resurrection on Mars Hill, he was met with mocking and scoffing (Acts 17:32). There were others in New Testament times who either doubted the doctrine or regarded the resurrection as purely spiritual (1 Cor. 15:12; 2 Tim. 2:18).

Evangelicals base their view of future resurrection upon the clear teaching of Scripture. They see implications and direct teaching of this doctrine in the Old Testament (Pss. 49:15; 73:24–25; Prov. 23:14; Job 19:25–27; Isa. 26:19; Dan. 12:2).

In the New Testament there is more teaching about the future resurrection of the dead. Jesus Himself argued for the resurrection in opposition to the Sadducees (Matt. 22:23–33). As He did so, He paralleled what he said with what the Old Testament declared (Ex. 3:6). In this way He appealed to the Old Testament to defend His own teaching.

On another occasion in reply to His critics, Jesus clearly set forth the doctrine of future resurrection from the dead. He said, ". . . the hour is coming in which all who are in the graves will hear His voice and come forth—those who have done good, to the resurrection of life, and those who have done evil, to the resurrection of condemnation" (John 5:28–29).

Repeatedly Jesus promised, "I will raise him up at the last day" to those who belonged to Him (John 6:39–40,

44, 54). He claimed to be "the resurrection and the life" (John 11:24–25).

On the basis of these and other passages of Scripture there is common agreement among evangelicals—all the dead will be raised at God's appointed time in the future. Again, regardless of other differences, all who name the name of Christ in truth can repeat the Apostles' Creed without a tongue-in-cheek attitude when it says, "I believe in the Resurrection of the body."

Future Divine Judgment

Nonevangelicals find it impossible to reconcile the doctrine of divine judgment with their concept of God, which is understandable since they reject so much of what the Bible says about Him. But evangelicals accept the authority of the Bible as well as the God of the Bible and therefore believe in divine judgment ahead.

Any concept of God as heavenly Father that compares him only to a lenient, permissive, earthly father is not true to the biblical presentation of Him. Indeed He is loving, gracious, and merciful; He is not a tyrant who rejoices in His judgment and punishment of sin. But God is also righteous and just and His love moved Him to make provision for sin in His Son. Rejection of Christ His Son means rejection of the only acceptable remedy for sin. Righteous wrath awaits all who reject God's Son as personal Savior.

That all men, as well as Satan and all the wicked angels, will one day stand before the God of the Bible in judgment is universally acknowledged by those who accept the Bible as God's Word. Conflict does not exist among evangelicals over this prophecy. The question among Christians is not, "Will God bring all to judgment?" They all agree that He will. This broad area of agreement is what we want to explore.

The agreement among evangelicals about the certainty of future divine judgment is not marred by their differences over the order of events. Their high view of God and His Word brings them all to the conclusion that divine judgment is ahead. True, God does judge sin in the present, but Scripture makes clear that these judgments of God experienced in the here and now are not final.

That all the unregenerate will one day appear before God in judgment is clear from John's record of the revelation God gave him:

> Then I saw a great white throne and Him who sat on it, from whose face the earth and the heaven fled away. And there was found no place for them. And I saw the dead, small and great, standing before God, and books were opened. And another book was opened, which is the Book of Life. And the dead were judged according to their works, by the things which were written in the books. The sea gave up the dead who were in it, and Death and Hades delivered up the dead who were in them. And they were judged, each one according to his works. Then Death and Hades were cast into the lake of fire. This is the second death. And anyone not found written in the Book of Life was cast into the lake of fire (Rev. 20:11–15).

Scripture is equally clear in its prophecy of the certainty of all believers standing personally and individually before God to give an account to Him. The apostle Paul reminded the Christians in Corinth and Rome of this.

To the Corinthians he wrote:

> Each one's work will become manifest; for the Day will declare it, because it will be revealed by fire; and the fire will test each one's work, of what sort it is. If anyone's work which he has built on it endures, he will receive a reward. If anyone's work is burned, he will suffer loss, but he himself will be saved, yet so as through fire (1 Cor. 3:13–15).

In his second letter to the same people he wrote, "For we must all appear before the judgement seat of Christ, that each one may receive the things done in the body, according to what he hath done, whether good or bad" (2 Cor. 5:10).

The Roman Christians were given the very same teaching:

> But why do you judge your brother? Or why do you show contempt for your brother? For we shall all stand before the judgment seat of Christ. For it is written: "As I live, says the LORD, every knee shall bow to Me and every tongue shall confess to God." So then each of us shall give account of himself to God (Rom. 14:10–12).

Final judgment also awaits the devil and his demons. The everlasting fire of hell was prepared for the devil and his angels (Matt. 25:41). In his vision, John was given to see "the devil, who deceived them, was cast into the lake of fire and brimstone where the beast and the false prophet are" (Rev. 20:10). There he is to be tormented day and night forever and ever.

Peter and Jude, both directed by the Holy Spirit, tell us of wicked angels being reserved in chains until the day of their final judgment (2 Peter 2:4; Jude 6).

Regardless of denominational affiliation, or lack of it, and in spite of whether one believes there will be one final judgment or whether there will be a number of different judgments separated by time, all evangelicals believe in future divine judgment. They take the words of the psalmist seriously and even literally and therefore as yet unfulfilled when he said, ". . . for He is coming to judge the earth. He shall judge the world with righteousness, And the peoples with His truth" (Ps. 96:13).

Future Return of Christ

The Old Testament prophets did not distinguish between the time of Christ's coming as a babe in Bethlehem's manger and His coming the second time in power and great glory. However, what they prophesied concerning Christ's coming is understood differently by evangelicals. Some see all the Old Testament prophecies of Christ's coming as already fulfilled in His first advent. Others believe a significant number of the prophecies await future fulfillment when He comes the second time.

Nevertheless, all Bible believers do agree that in the New Testament we have clear prophecy of Christ coming to the earth again. Jesus and the writers of the New Testament agree; His first coming will be followed by a second one.

Those who witnessed Christ's ascension heard the angelic messengers say, "Men of Galilee, why do you stand gazing up into heaven? This same Jesus, who was taken up from you into heaven, will so come in like manner as you saw Him go into heaven" (Acts 1:11).

Long before He returned to the Father, Jesus taught His followers that He would come again. As He sat on the

Mount of Olives, He told His disciples about the future. They were warned of difficult times ahead and were assured of their Lord's return:

> For then there will be great tribulation, such as has not been since the beginning of the world until this time, no, nor ever shall be. And unless those days were shortened, no flesh would be saved; but for the elect's sake those days will be shortened. Then if anyone says to you, "Look here is the Christ!" or "There!" do not believe it. For false christs and false prophets will rise and show great signs and wonders to deceive, if possible, even the elect. See, I have told you beforehand. Therefore if they say to you, "Look, He is in the desert!" do not go out; or "Look, He is in the inner rooms!" do not believe it. For as the lightning comes from the east and flashes to the west, so also will the coming of the Son of Man be (Matt. 24:21–27).

In what has come to be called Christ's Upper Room Discourse, He brought comfort to His disciples by announcing that He would come again for them. They had been told but did not want to think about His death and to encourage them Jesus said, "I will come again and receive you to Myself" (John 14:3).

Even the very last book in the Bible holds out the promise of Christ's second coming. John, in a vision, saw Christ whose name is called "The Word of God," coming from heaven to earth along with the armies of heaven (Rev. 19:11–16).

It makes no difference whether they embrace the amillennial, the postmillennial, or premillennial scheme, evangelicals all agree the predictions of Christ's future return have not yet been realized. Will Christ come first in the air for all His children (1 Thess. 4:13–18)? Is this coming to be distinguished from His coming to the earth (Rev. 19:11–16)? Evangelicals have different answers to such questions but they all agree that Christ is coming to the earth again just as surely as He came the first time.

What have we discovered thus far in our study? We have seen that despite differences over details, evangelicals agree on several major issues regarding prophecy of things to come. They all agree mankind lives on after death and that heaven as well as hell will be occupied by humans. There will be a new heaven and a new earth in the future. All of God's creatures will face Him in judgment. The dead, small and great, will be raised to spend eternity either with God in heaven or with the devil in hell. Christ is coming back to this earth again and His future coming will be just as literal as when He came as a babe in Bethlehem's manger.

We evangelicals have so much in common and some of these major areas of agreement have been explored. The great fundamentals of the faith bind us together in the family of God and set us apart from those who reject the inspiration and authority of the Bible. One of these fundamentals is the doctrine of the future bodily return of Christ. Fellowship in the things of the Lord that we hold in common should characterize our lives, not fights over details of unfulfilled prophecy.

The Eternal State

Evangelicals all believe heaven and hell are real places and human beings will dwell forever in one or the other of these places. The Bible plainly says both exist and will be occupied by humans throughout eternity.

Critical biblical scholarship tells us we can no longer believe the pre-Copernican view of the universe. Science, we are told, has disproved belief in a three-decker universe, which was a common belief about the time the Bible was being written. Modern science insists that the sun, not the earth, is the center of our galaxy. Therefore, up is no longer really up for earthdwellers, and down is no longer down.

Such views were bound to make an impact upon theological thinking sooner or later, and so they did. Rudolf Bultmann expressed his unbelief in the Bible's view of heaven and hell this way:

> Man's knowledge and mastery of the world have advanced to such an extent that through science and technology it is no longer possible for anyone seriously to hold a New Testament view of the world—in fact, there is no one who does. . . . No one who is old enough to think for himself supposes that God lives in a local heaven. There is no longer any heaven in the traditional sense of the word. The same applies to hell in the sense of any mythical underworld beneath our feet. And if this is so, we can no longer accept the story of Christ's descent into hell or His Ascension into Heaven as literally true. We can no longer look for the return of the Son of Man on the clouds of heaven or hope that the faithful will meet him in the air (1 Thess. 4:15ff).[6]

As far as most of modern science is concerned, truth does not exist outside the scientific realm. The supernatural, the miraculous is denied by unbelieving scientists and consequently by much of modern theology as well.

In response to the contention that we can no longer accept the Bible's teaching that heaven and hell are real places and remain intellectually honest, Lesley Woodson made this observation,

> What is so often overlooked is that there are different truth dimensions and truth in one of these dimensions need not be denied by truth in another. Their natures are not the same. Thus one can be intellectually honest while embracing both the Copernican view of the physical world and a three-decker view of the metaphysical world at one and the same time.[7]

Time will not go on forever! This is another point of agreement among Bible believers. Eternity is as much a certainty for evangelicals as time is now present reality. If the Bible does not teach this, it does not teach anything. (When time will end and eternity begin is another question however.) That there is a future world out there is not disputed by God's people. No believing student of the Scripture accepts the notion that death ends it all.

True biblical teaching of both heaven and hell is often neglected today. Heaven and hell are also frequently misrepresented. Modern man often uses the biblical terminology but invests it with new meaning. For example, experiences of a hard life are sometimes described as "hell on earth" and the person who is deprived of the essential things, or even just the good things of life, is said to be "going through hell." Ron Devillier gave this description of hell:

> Hell is where the poor are trapped in the ghetto of indifference. It is the high school campus where some persons are socially crippled because they do not fit. It is the back section of a psychiatric ward of a charity hospital where the bruised ones that did not get enough love are hidden. It is a small village in Vietnam where people

> lay in the streets, victims of a stray bomb. It is a dingy jail downtown where frightened human beings cower. It is a small town high school where a teenage girl returns from a home for unwed mothers after giving birth to her child. It is a street of charred buildings, broken windows, and looted stores—the aftermath of a riot—kindled by frustration, hopelessness, and rage.[8]

Devillier may have a biblical view of hell all right, but his words in this instance do not reveal it. To be sure, those who go through the experiences he described are, no doubt, having the nearest thing to "hell on earth," but the Bible tells us that there is a hell far worse than anything possible on this earth. No amount of misfortune and poverty, and all that goes with them, even begin to compare with the horrors and torments of hell. Those who reject the Lord Jesus Christ as their personal Savior will go to a place of eternal torment that the Bible calls the "lake of fire."

Because the Bible teaches it, evangelicals believe in an eternal existence for man, either in heaven or hell. Prophecy concerning man's existence in these two abodes, and the bliss or torment to be encountered there are rarely disputed by evangelicals. They accept at face value Scripture's clear teaching on these issues.

Concerning heaven, Jesus said, "I go to prepare a place for you" (John 14:2). He told them plainly He wanted them with Him in this place He would prepare and that He would receive them there.

Hell, Jesus taught, was also a real place promising eternal torment for the devil and his angels, as well as the sons and daughters of Adam who rejected Him and His sacrifice for their sins. He called it a place of "damnation" where "the fire is not quenched" (Matt. 23:33; Mark 9:48 KJV). There is an abundance of other Scripture teaching the same thing in addition, of course, to what Jesus said about heaven and hell as eternal abodes.

Evangelicals agree too, that there will be a new heaven and a new earth in the future. The prophet Isaiah wrote of these. He recorded Jehovah's answer to the prayer of the believing remnant. In part the answer was "For behold, I create new heavens and a new earth; and the former shall not be remembered or come to mind" (Isa. 65:17). " 'For as the new heavens and the new earth which I will make shall remain before Me,' says the LORD, 'so shall your descendants and your name remain' "(Isa. 66:22).

In New Testament times, Peter was still predicting judgment upon the present heavens and earth (2 Peter 3:7). He also said, "The heavens will pass away with a great noise, and the elements will melt with fervent heat; both the earth and the works that are in it will be burned up" (v. 10). But he prophesied further, "We . . . look for new heavens and a new earth in which righteousness dwells" (v. 13). John in his apocalyptic vision saw Christ on a throne and from his "face the earth and the heaven fled away" (Rev. 20:11). Also the beloved disciple "saw a new heaven and a new earth" (Rev. 21:1).

The present heavens and earth have not yet been "destroyed." Prophecy that they will awaits future fulfillment, and so does the prophecy of the creation of the new heaven and the new earth. Bible believers do not differ over such things. They agree that the eternal state has not yet begun.

In the next chapter, we will present the different evangelical viewpoints with regard to how and in what order these future happenings will take place. There are a number of variations in the sequence and details accompanying these major unfulfilled prophecies. Study of these will get us close to the actual warfare, some of it fierce and with rancor and often without regard to any rules relative to Christian ethics. This is to our shame.

For Further Thought

1. Why do evangelicals agree on the major essentials of eschatology?
2. Do you believe in heaven? Hell?
3. Do you know why some evangelicals insist all the dead will be raised and judged at the same time?
4. Do you know why some evangelicals believe strongly that there will be no such thing as a general resurrection and judgment?
5. On what basis do evangelicals agree that Christ will come again to the earth?

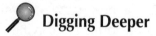 **Digging Deeper**

Those who believe in a future resurrection and a final judgment generally agree that there is a state of existence between this life and the resurrection but not on the conditions surrounding that intermediate state. The doctrine of purgatory advanced by the Roman Catholic Church is rejected by evangelical protestants because they do not believe it has any biblical support. In the history of the church it was not until the middle of the fifteenth century that the Latin branch of the church denounced a view common within ancient Judaism, the idea that believers were in a semiconscious state between death and resurrection. Soul sleep between death and resurrection is embraced by Jehovah's Witnesses and Seventh-Day Adventists, but this, too, is rejected by mainline evangelicalism.

Evangelicals differ most over whether or not there is an intermediate body for the believer in the intermediate state. The major passage of Scripture dealing with this matter is 2 Corinthians 5:1–3. For further study on this question I recommend two excellent sources. Loraine Boettner's *Immortality* (Philadelphia: The Presbyterian and Reformed Publishing Co., 1962) has a good section on the intermediate state. A scholarly defense of the belief in an intermediate body for believers is also found in Greg Enos's Th.D. Dissertation, "To Die Is Gain: The Christian's Intermediate State" (Dallas: Dallas Theological Seminary, 1989).

Another area in which the reader may want to dig deeper is the current controversy among evangelicals over the eternal destiny of the unsaved. "Biblical universalism" or "qualified universalism" describes the view that comes between the view of eternal torment for the unregenerate and universalism. Some evangelicals are seeking to defend the view that God assigns those who have not responded to the gospel to an irrevocable and definite death. They believe the "fire" of hell does not torment eternally. Rather it consumes the wicked. In other words, they are advocating that it is the death that is everlasting punishment rather than the torment.

For further study on this and related issues see the

extended article by Roger Nicole, Neal Punt, Clark Pinnock, Kenneth Kantzer, and David Wells, entitled "Universalism: Will Everyone Be Saved?" in *Christianity Today* (March 20, 1987) and Jon E. Braun's book *Whatever Happened to Hell!* (Nashville: Thomas Nelson Publishers, 1979).

Part 2

SYSTEMS OF ESCHATOLOGY: HOW EVANGELICALS DIFFER

3

Premillennialism

Systems of Eschatology

Three major evangelical systems of thought, as we have noted, offer explanations of God's plan of procedure for the future. Since they are evangelical, the adherents of each view accept biblical authority and seek to be true to the meaning of God's Word. Dedicated men and women who love the Lord and His Word hold these views and their honesty and sincerity should not be questioned. But all three systems cannot fully represent the biblical teaching because they are so different and in conflict with each other.

Each millennial system has a different picture of what will take place when Christ returns to the earth. Will Christ return after the church has christianized the world? Will He establish an earthly kingdom and reign for one thousand years on David's throne in Jerusalem? Or will the eternal state be ushered in at His second coming?

Other sharp distinctions exist between the major interpretations of things to come but basic to them all are the questions: Will Christ institute the Davidic kingdom on earth? Will the church succeed in Christianizing society before Christ returns? Will He usher in the eternal state when He comes again?

The three systems of thought need to be presented along with important variations that are true of each. Little will be said for or against them. Our purpose here is simply to expose the reader to the different views of unfulfilled prophecy as held by evangelicals.

Nonevangelicals or nonconservatives of all religious varieties usually have such a weak view of the Bible and its authority that they find no difficulty dealing with prophecy the way they deal with most of the Bible—reject it, and treat it as myth or as purely symbolic without literal meaning at all. In short, they do not take Scripture seriously.

An example of the liberal view will show the contrast with evangelical belief. C. H. Dodd in his *The Parables of the Kingdom,* made famous the phrase "realized eschatology." In general, all nonevangelicals agree with Dodd in his view of the unfulfilled prophecies: "The eschaton has moved from the future to the present, from the sphere of expectation into that of realized experience."[1]

According to his view, all eschatology—the doctrine of future things—was fulfilled at the Incarnation of Christ. Dodd arrives at his view by a process of wholesale discrediting of Scripture. With apparent ease he calls much of the Bible fraudulent. What is not fraudulent, he either explains away or distorts to fit his presuppositions and even goes so far as to say that Christ was simply mistaken in some of His prophecies. In other words the Lord Jesus Christ was wrong.

But among those who accept the divine authority of Holy Scripture and who do, therefore, take it seriously, three totally different views about the future program of God for mankind and the world persist. The distinctions between these systems of belief are by no means imaginary or unimportant. To the contrary, there are far-reaching consequences associated with each of the views. These views will now be presented in the order they arose and developed in the history of the church.

Premillennialism

The word *millennium* comes from the Latin words *mille* meaning thousand and *annus* meaning year. Though not found in the Bible, the Greek equivalent of millennium appears six times in Revelation 20. A designated period of time is meant by the word. Belief in such a period of time has been called chiliasm or millennarianism. The prefix *pre* before the word *millennium* means before. Thus premillennialism describes the belief that Christ will return before the millennium and in fact will establish it when He returns to the earth.

The future 1000-year Millennium will be characterized by righteousness (Isa. 60:21), holiness (Isa. 52:10), truth (Ps. 45:4), and the fullness of the Holy Spirit of God (Joel 2:28–29). Christ will rule and reign from His throne in Jerusalem over the whole world. Satan will be bound in the abyss for the entire period (Rev. 20:1–6). During that time all war will cease (Isa. 9:4–7), and there will be joy (Isa. 9:3–4), peace (Isa. 65:25), holiness (Isa. 1:26–27), glory (Isa. 24:23), comfort (Isa. 12:1–2), perfect justice (Isa. 9:7), the lifting of the curse imposed because of sin and the removal of sickness (Isa. 33:24), healing of the deformed (Isa. 29:17–19), great economic prosperity (Isa. 25:1–2), unified worship of God (Isa. 45:23), and the visible manifestation of the very presence of God Himself (Ezek. 37:27–28).

A distinguished defender of the premillennial system of thought defined it this way:

> In general, the premillennial system may be characterized as follows: Premillennialists believe that theirs is the historic faith of the church holding to a literal interpretation of the Scriptures, they believe that the promises made to Abraham and David are unconditional and have had or will have a literal fulfillment. In no sense have these promises made to Israel been abrogated or fulfilled by the Church which is a distinct body in this age having promises and a destiny different from Israel's. At the close of this age, premillennialists believe that Christ will return for His church meeting her in the air (this is not the Second Coming of Christ), which event called the rapture or translation, will usher in a seven-year period of Tribulation on the earth. After this the Lord will return to the earth (this is the Second Coming of Christ), to establish His kingdom on the earth for one thousand years during which time the promises to Israel will be fulfilled.[2]

It is generally agreed by students of the early church that premillennialism was the view held by many in the post-apostolic age. That it is the oldest of the three millennial views is seldom debated, but age of course, does not necessarily mean accuracy. The view prevailed and was virtually unchallenged until the time of Origen (185–254) and his allegorical or nonliteral method of interpretation of

Scripture. The basic reason for the three millennial views is the method used by each system in its interpretation of those passages of Scripture dealing with unfulfilled prophecy. More will be said about this later.

Premillennialism went into something of an eclipse from the time of Origen until about 1830 and the time of the prophetic Bible conferences when it was revived. During the intervening years, amillennialism, to be studied later, was the prevailing system of belief.

Differences among Premillenialists

Premillennialists all agree that when Christ returns to the earth, He will institute the kingdom promised to David. Christ's second coming in power and great glory is not followed immediately by the eternal state. Instead, the one-thousand-year earthly rule of Christ begins at that time. Old Testament promises to Israel will then be fulfilled, and the covenants God made with Abraham (Gen. 12) and David (2 Sam. 7) will then be realized.

Is there going to be, in the future, a seven-year period of unprecedented tribulation that will be the outpouring of God's wrath upon the world? Will this be what Jeremiah called "the time of Jacob's trouble" (Jer. 30:7), a time of divine judgment unlike any other? Did Jesus refer to this time when He told His disciples there would be a "great tribulation, such as has not been since the beginning of the world until this time, no, nor ever shall be" (Matt. 24:21)?

Premillennialists are in general agreement in answering "yes" to these questions.

Will the church, the body of Christ, be called upon to go through the seven-year period of tribulation? Premillennialists are not all agreed on the order in which some of the future events will transpire and give different answers to this question. For example, there are at least four different views of the relation of the church, which is Christ's body, to the coming tribulation.

The Church To Be Raptured before the Tribulation Begins

Some believe the entire church will be raptured, caught up to be with the Lord, before any part of the future seven-year Tribulation begins. Those who hold this view are called pretribulationists.

The future seven-year period of unprecedented tribulation will be characterized by global wars, famine, death, anarchy, hail, and fire mixed with blood burning up one-third of the trees and all green grass, whole mountains burning with fire, one-third of the seas becoming blood, water resources becoming bitter as gall, darkness in the skies during the daylight hours, scorpion plague tormenting but not killing, painful-sores plague, death of all sea life, sun scorching humans with fire, earthquakes, and catastrophic earth and heaven revolutions (cf. Rev. 6—16).

John F. Walvoord, a widely recognized authority and spokesman for premillennial pretribulationalism, defined the position this way:

> The pretribulational interpretation regards the coming of the Lord and the translation of the church as preceding immediately the fulfillment of Daniel's prophecy of a final seven-year period before the second advent. Based on a literal interpretation of Daniel's prophecy, it is held that there has been no fulfillment of Daniel 9:27 in his-

tory and that therefore it prophesies a future period, familiarly called "the tribulation." The seven years of Daniel, bringing to a close the program of Israel prior to the second advent, will, therefore, be fulfilled between the translation of the church and the second advent of Christ to establish His kingdom on earth. At the translation, before the seven years, Christ will return to meet the church in the air; at the second advent after the seven years, it is held that Christ will return with His church from heaven to establish His millennial reign on earth.[3]

Despite a number of similarities, pretribulationists find a definite distinction in Scripture between God's program with Israel and His program with the church. They also see a difference between Christ's coming *for* His own and His coming *with* His own. The coming *for* His own they call the "Rapture"; Christ's coming *with* His own to the earth is called the "Second Coming." At least one thousand years for the earthly reign of Christ and seven years of tribulation on the earth come between the Rapture and the Second Coming in this view.

Pretribulationists are also dispensationalists. A dispensationalist sees a clear distinction in the Bible between God's program with the nation Israel and His program with the church. Dispensationalists believe the church began on the Day of Pentecost as a distinct entity from Israel. According to dispensationalists, God has dealt differently with His people at different times. They teach that there has always been only one way of salvation, however—by grace through faith and altogether apart from human works. Even though dispensationalists cannot find their system clearly delineated in the early history of the church, they insist its basic tenets are to be found there.

It is generally agreed that a dispensation is "a distinguishable economy in the outworking of God's purpose."[4] The dispensational system of biblical interpretation may be described this way:

> Dispensationalism views the world as a household run by God. In this household-world, God is dispensing or administering its affairs according to His own will and in various stages of revelation in the process of time. These various stages mark off the distinguishably different economies in the outworking of His total purpose and these economies are the dispensations. The understanding of God's differing economies is essential to a proper interpretation of His revelation within those various economies.[5]

Basic to the pretribulational view is belief in Christ's imminent return, that He could come at any time. In other words, there are no prophecies awaiting fulfillment before His return in the air for His own. Among premillennial pretribulationists there is general agreement on the order of major events in the future. A listing of these will be helpful in understanding the view.

1. Increase in apostasy as this age draws to a close (1 Tim. 4:1–3; 2 Tim. 3:1–5).
2. Resurrection of the dead in Christ or those saved in this age, accompanied by the translation of the living saints and the rapture of both groups (1 Cor. 15:20–24, 35–50; 1 Thess. 4:13–18).
3. The seven-year Tribulation on earth (Rev. 6—16). Those resurrected and translated earlier are with the Lord in heaven. The judgment seat of Christ (1 Cor. 3:12–15) and the marriage of the Lamb take

place (Rev. 19:7) while the Tribulation judgments are poured out on earth.

4. The Battle of Armageddon and the end of the Tribulation. Christ comes with His own to the earth (Rev. 19:11–16). When Christ comes, Israel will be regathered and judged (Matt. 24:37—25:46). The Gentile nations will also be judged (Matt. 25:31–46).

5. The millennial reign of Christ begins. It will be one thousand years in length (Rev. 20:1–6). Before it begins, however, Satan is bound in the bottomless pit (Rev. 20:1). After the one-thousand-year reign, Satan will be loosed for a little season (Rev. 20:7). He will deceive the nations and lead a revolt against God, be defeated by Christ, and then cast into the lake of fire where he will remain forever (Rev. 20:10).

6. The Great White Throne Judgment (Rev. 20:11–15) occurs at which all the unsaved of all the ages appear and are afterward cast into the lake of fire.

7. Creation of a new heaven and a new earth (Rev. 21:1).

8. Eternity (Rev. 22:1–6).

The Premillennial Pretribulation View (Chart 5) depicts the basic view now under discussion.[6] This is the most prominent view among premillennialists.

The Church To Go Through the Tribulation

Some who insist they are premillennial have raised serious questions about the belief that the church will es-

Lord descends with a shout, trumpet of God.

Second Coming of Christ, when He destroys the lawless one (2 Thess. 2:8)

Church raptured, dead in Christ rise first (1 Thess. 4:15–18).

the church on earth

7-year Tribulation on earth

1,000-year reign of Christ on earth

CHURCH AGE   TRIBULATION   MILLENNIUM

Premillennial Pretribulation Rapture

Chart 5

cape the future seven-year Tribulation. They do not believe the church will be raptured or caught up to meet the Lord in the air before the Tribulation begins on earth. Rather, it is their contention that the church must pass through the period called "the time of Jacob's distress" in Scripture, or future seven-year Tribulation on earth. They insist God will protect or preserve His own through this time. This view is called posttribulationism and is common among amillennialists and postmillennialists but is also held by some premillennialists.

Alexander Reese, an advocate of the view, gave this definition of premillennial posttribulationism:

> The Church of Christ will not be removed from the earth until the advent of Christ at the very end of the present Age: the Rapture and the Appearing take place at the same crisis; hence Christians of that generation will be exposed to the final affliction under Antichrist.[7]

Considerable differences exist among evangelicals who are posttribulational. Those who do not subscribe to premillennialism believe the Tribulation began with the early church.[8] Some even say it began with Adam.[9] But posttribulationists who are premillennial take Scripture that speaks of great tribulation (Jer. 30:7; Dan. 12:1; Matt. 24:21) as unfulfilled and yet to be fulfilled in the future.[10]

As can be seen from Reese's definition above, the premillennial posttribulationists' position makes little distinction between Christ's coming *for* His own in the Rapture and His coming to the earth *with* His own to establish the kingdom. Distinction between God's program for Israel and His program for the church is even less marked. The hope that Christ could come at any time is either denied or redefined.

Posttribulationists are not dispensational[11] and they do not generally present a detailed order of future events. We may safely say, however, that they all believe the church will go through the coming Tribulation. Christ's coming *for* His own and coming *with* His own will be at the same time and a general resurrection and general judgment of all men and evil angels will occur before the eternal state begins. The Premillennial Posttribulational Rapture (Chart 6) pictures this position.

Premillennial Posttribulation Rapture

Chart 6

The Church To Go Through the First Half of the Tribulation

There are also some premillennialists who believe the church will pass through half of the future Tribulation. The last half of the seventieth week mentioned in Daniel 9:24–27 is seen to be far more severe than the first half. This view has the church raptured in the middle of the week or in the middle of the Tribulation and is known as the midtribulational view. It is a relatively new explanation of the relation of the church to the coming Tribulation. Midtribulationists do not usually use the term midtribulation to refer to themselves. They consider themselves pretribulational since they do believe Christ will return to rapture His own before what they call the great Tribulation or the last half of Daniel's seventieth week.[12]

Gleason L. Archer, who holds the position, gave this description of the view:

> Between the competing views of the pretribulation and the posttribulation rapture stands a mediating option, the theory of the mid-seventieth week rapture. Some refer to it as the midtribulation rapture as though the sudden deliverance of the Church were to take place after the first three and a half years of the final seven before the return of Christ to establish His kingdom on earth. But if the great tribulation is regarded as commencing with the outpouring of the wrath of God on the world as described in Revelation 16—18, then it is hardly accurate to describe the mid-week view as a midtribulation theory, for it is really a form of pretribulation rapturism which limits the time interval climatic world suffering to the final three and a half years prior to the battle of Armageddon. To me, this approach seems to offer fewer problems than either of the other views.[13]

To a certain extent the divine programs with Israel and the church seem to overlap in this viewpoint. This is because the church participates in at least part of the Tribulation called "the time of Jacob's trouble," and the seventieth week of Daniel, but not the most severe judgments of the period.

As can be noted in the Premillennial Midtribulational Rapture (Chart 7) the order of events for the future is basically the same in the midtribulation view as in the pretribulational position.

Lord descends with a shout, trumpet of God.

Second Coming of Christ, when He destroys the lawless one (2 Thess. 2:8)

Church raptured, dead in Christ rise first (1 Thess. 4:15–18).

3¹/₂-year Tribulation on earth includes the church.

3¹/₂-year Tribulation on earth

1,000-year reign of Christ on earth

CHURCH AGE AND FIRST PART OF TRIBULATION

LAST PART OF TRIBULATION

MILLENNIUM

Premillennial Midtribulation Rapture

Chart 7

The Prewrath Rapture of the Church

This view, though similar to the midtribulational view, is also different in some ways. The similarity is that it also sees the church in the first part of Daniel's seventieth week (Dan. 9:24–27). Neither of the views has the church raptured before that "week" of seven years begins.

The prewrath view is different from the midtribulational view in that it does not have the Rapture exactly in the middle of the week. Midtribulationism places the Rapture with the sounding of the seventh trumpet (Rev. 11) while prewrath rapturism places it with the sounding of the first trumpet and at the same time as the Second Coming which is before the Day of the Lord begins.

The prewrath Rapture view is at this time a minority view. It has been embraced and popularized by Marvin Rosenthal who was the executive director of the Friends of Israel Ministries for 16 years. He and this organization staunchly defended the pretribulational Rapture view until his recent change. He is no longer a part of the Friends of Israel Ministries. Rosenthal's book *The Prewrath Rapture of the Church* (Nashville, Tenn.: Thomas Nelson, 1990) sets forth the view and its defense.

In brief it may be said that the view is built on the basic assumption that the seal judgments (Rev. 6) do not represent the wrath of God. The divine wrath begins with the trumpet judgments introduced by cataclysmic disturbances. Also, the view places the church within the Olivet Discourse as given by Jesus in Matthew 24 and 25.

Rosenthal does have the entire church involved in the Rapture. The Rapture takes place eighteen months before the seven-year Tribulation comes to an end. The Second Coming is initiated by the Rapture which brings God's wrath on earth dwellers. This will all culminate at the Battle of Armageddon and will be followed by the millennial reign of Christ.

The prewrath Rapture view is different from the normal premillennial view in that it does not consistently distinguish between God's program with Israel and His program with the church. The ways it differs are that it has the church in Israel's seventieth week and does not hold to the doctrine of imminency.

The chart that follows has been adapted from *The Prewrath Rapture of the Church* and shows how the view sees end-time events.

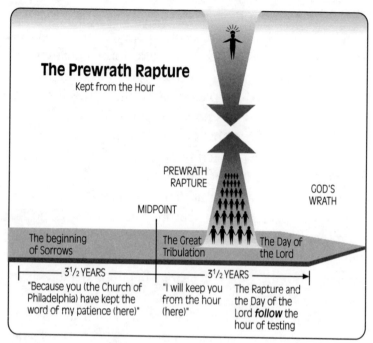

Chart 8

Only Spiritual Believers to Be Raptured Before the Tribulation Begins

The major difference between this view and the pretribulational view is the number of believers who will be raptured when Christ returns. Partial rapturism is the name of this interpretation.

A contemporary exponent of the view presented three purposes for the future Tribulation. It is to be a time of trouble for Israel and a means of destroying the wicked:

> Finally, we would note that the purpose of the tribulation
> is also to be the testing of lukewarm shallow Laodicean

Christians who will be left behind at the coming of Christ. No doubt multitudes who expected to be raptured will be disappointed because like the foolish virgins, they were not watchful. Tribulation is then for the purpose of trying the faith of these who profess to be Christians but who really never repented or are living in disobedience to the will of God.[14]

According to partial rapturism only those Christians who are ready for the Lord are raptured when He comes. One is made ready for that great event by living a spiritual life and being watchful for Christ's return. Believers reveal their readiness by looking for the Lord while those who are not living spiritual lives will not be prepared and raptured

Lord descends with a shout, trumpet of God.

Second Coming of Christ, when He destroys the lawless one (2 Thess. 2:8)

"Spiritual" Christians raptured (Matt. 25:1–13), dead in Christ rise first (1 Thess. 4:15–18).

1,000-year reign of Christ on earth

the church on earth

7-year Tribulation on earth includes "carnal" Christians.

CHURCH AGE   TRIBULATION   MILLENNIUM

Premillennial Pretribulation Partial Rapture

Chart 9

when spiritual Christians are. They will be left to go through at least some of the Tribulation so that they will be made ready to meet their Lord.

The Premillennial Pretribulation Partial Rapture View (Chart 9) shows that the order of future events in this position is the same as that of the pretribulation order given earlier except that some Christians remain to go into the Tribulation for purposes of cleansing.

4

Amillennialism

The prefix *a* means *no*. Amillennialism is the view that does not believe in a future literal reign of Christ on earth for a thousand years in fulfillment of the Old Testament promises of God.

One of its advocates, J. G. Voss, has defined it this way:

> Amillennialism is that view of the last things which holds the Bible does not predict a "millennium" or period of world-wide peace and righteousness on this earth before the end of the world. Amillennialism teaches that there will be a parallel in contemporaneous development of good and evil—God's Kingdom and Satan's kingdom—in this world which will continue until the second coming of Christ. At the second coming of Christ, the resurrection and judgment will take place, followed by the eternal order of things—the absolute, perfect kingdom of God, in which there will be no sin, suffering, nor death.[1]

Jay Adams, who embraces the amillennial interpretation, calls the term amillennialism an unhappy one. He does not believe it really describes the position accurately.

> *Amillennialism* is not only a misnomer because it is neg-
> ative, but the distinction which it makes is a false one.
> No amillennialist denies that the Bible teaches a millen-
> nium. But the word *amillennialism* means no millen-
> nium. The issue is not whether Revelation 20 teaches a
> millennium. All amillennialists believe it does. . . . The
> true difference between amillennialism and the other
> systems involves two things:
>
> 1. The nature of the millennium.
> 2. The chronological position of the millennium
>   in the economy of God.
>
> The word *amillennialism* fails to draw either of these dis-
> tinctions. Instead it expresses the belief which no conser-
> vative holds—that there is no millennium. The term can-
> not be defended and certainly should be abandoned.
> Amillennialists simply are not amillennialists.[2]

A new term is suggested by Adams to refer to the position that he embraces and that has been known historically as amillennialism:

> Accurately speaking the biblical system may be distin-
> guished from the other systems as *realized millennial-
> ism.* Whereas both pre and postmillennialists look for-
> ward to a future unrealized millennium, realized
> millennialists contend that the millennium is a present
> reality. This chronological difference necessarily involves
> the *nature* of the period. If the millennium is a present
> reality, it is most certainly of the non-utopian type. Both
> of the other systems maintain that the millennium is fu-
> ture exactly *because* they cannot conceive of its nature
> as identical with the present church age. Both wrongly
> look for an earthly utopia apart from that fiery purging
> which alone will bring what the Bible calls "the new
> earth." They anticipate a golden age prior to the judg-
> ment of all men. Adherents to *realized* millennialism, on

the other hand, maintain that such a belief confounds the millennium with the eternal state described in the last two chapters of Revelation; 2 Peter 3:12–14; Isaiah 65:17, and other prophecies. While *realized* millennialists believe there is a future golden age, they teach that it follows the millennial period. It will not come until the old earth has "fled away" (Rev. 20:11).[3]

Perhaps the term realized millennialism is a better description of the position traditionally known as amillennialism, but be that as it may, the fact still remains that this interpretation does not allow for a future earthly kingdom with Christ ruling from David's throne in Jerusalem. In that way, it is distinct from premillennialism and postmillennialism.

Amillennialists all reject dispensationalism. They believe it is a rather recent human invention foisted upon the Scriptures. In place of dispensational theology amillennialists, and postmillennialists for that matter, have traditionally substituted what is known as covenant theology.[4] "It represents the whole of Scripture as being covered by two covenants: (1) the covenant of works; (2) the covenant of grace."[5]

The covenant of works was an agreement between God and Adam where God promised life for obedience or death for disobedience. Adam and mankind in him failed, so to save man from the penalty of his disobedience, the covenant of grace became operative. This is the agreement between the offended God and the offending elect sinner in which God promises salvation through Christ. A covenant of redemption, or, the agreement in eternity past between the Father, Son, and Holy Spirit as to each one's

Theological Covenants

Covenant of Redemption
between Father, Son, and Spirit

Father

GOD

Son   Spirit

Covenant of Works
between God and Adam

Adam

GOD

Elect
Sinners

Covenant of Grace
betwen God and elect sinners

Chart 10

part in the redemptive plan of God, is also usually included in the system. See the Theological Covenants
(Chart 10) for the relation of these to each other.

The covenants in covenant theology—redemption,
works, grace—must not be confused with the covenants
such as the Abrahamic and Davidic stressed by dispensationalists. In covenant theology, these biblical covenants
are subservient to the covenant of grace. Dispensationalism, on the other hand, places primary emphasis upon the
biblical covenants though it doesn't deny the covenants in
covenant theology. In other words, covenant theology and
dispensationalism are built upon entirely different foundations. The former understands the Bible on the basis of the

Four Biblical Covenants

ABRAHAMIC
Genesis
12:1–3

LAND   SEED   BLESSING

PALESTINIAN	DAVIDIC	NEW
Deuteronomy	2 Samuel	Jeremiah
30:1–10	7:12–16	31:31–34

Chart 11

covenant of grace and the latter, to be discussed later, interprets it more from the perspective of the Abrahamic, Davidic, Palestinian, and New covenants. See the Four Biblical Covenants (Chart 11) for their relation to each other.

Amillennialism is not without division in its ranks. The division comes over the exact way to interpret Scripture verses that seem to describe a millennium. Some follow St. Augustine (354–430) and see the Millennium as being fulfilled now on earth. See St. Augustine's Amillennial View (Chart 12).

Others, following B. B. Warfield's lead, believe the promises of a millennium are being fulfilled in heaven now. This is the more contemporary view. See the diagram

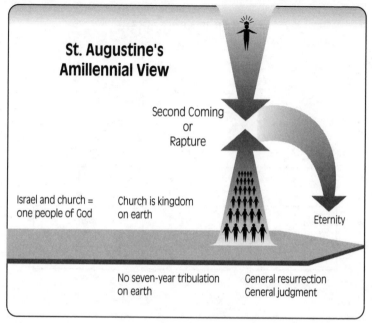

Chart 12

on Warfield's Amillennial View (Chart 13).

Both groups agree that Christ will come again literally and bodily. When He comes a second time He will not institute a kingdom on earth but instead will usher in the eternal state.

Regardless of whether the church is viewed as the kingdom on earth or whether the kingdom promises are being fulfilled in heaven now, the future order of events is the same in amillennialism. Either way there is no future for Israel as a nation. God's promises to His people were conditional and, since the conditions were not met, they have been abrogated or, according to some amillennialists, transferred and are now being fulfilled by the church.

Warfield's Amillennial View

Kingdom promises fulfilled now in heaven

Second Coming or Rapture

Israel and church = one people of God

Church is not the kingdom on earth

Eternity

No seven-year tribulation on earth

General resurrection General judgment

Chart 13

The future order of events embraced by most evangelical amillennialists is:

1. Worsening conditions in the world before the Second Coming,
2. The Second Coming of Christ accompanied by,
3. The general resurrection and general judgment followed by,
4. Eternity.

Conclusive evidence for widespread amillennialism in the first two centuries of the Christian church seems to be lacking. With the rise of the allegorical interpretation of Scripture in the third century, amillennialism came into existence and flourished.

Augustine seems to be the first theologian of any stature to embrace the amillennial system of theology. He argued that the church was the kingdom on earth. The hermeneutic he employed was the allegorical and nonliteral method of interpretation applied to prophecy. He systematized and applied to prophecy the hermeneutical (interpretational) method supplied by Origen before him. The allegorical or spiritualizing method of interpretation is the method that uses the normal or literal method as a vehicle to get to a deeper, more profound meaning, after which the literal method and meaning are discarded.

Evangelicals, however, who embrace the amillennial view of things to come employ a less than literal method of interpretation only in certain unfulfilled prophecies. (More will be said about the interpretation of Scripture in the next chapter because nothing is more basic to the understanding of prophecy.)

The Roman Catholic Church fully embraced the Augustinian variety of amillennialism from the very beginning. The great Protestant Reformers did the same. Their chief interest, however, was not with prophecy and future and final events. Salvation by faith alone and the authority of the Bible alone were the primary concerns of the Reformers and they seldom or never discussed eschatology.

Amillennialism continued to flourish until the time of Daniel Whitby (1638–1726) and the rise of postmillennialism. For some time the postmillennial view prevailed and amillennialism was in abeyance. When World War II shattered postmillennialism's optimistic outlook, amillennialism came back into prominence again, but in a slightly different version.

The Augustinian tradition that said the church was the kingdom on earth was rejected. In its place came the view that the Millennium is distinct from the church after all. Christ's kingdom was said to be heavenly, not earthly. The kingdom promises in the Bible were said to be fulfilled in the state of blessedness of the saints in heaven and Christ's position at the right hand of the Father. In other words, Christ's present position was seen as the fulfillment of the kingdom promises in the Old Testament. This is the most common variety of amillennialism held by evangelicals today.

5

Postmillennialism

According to this system, Christ will return after society has been Christianized by the church. In this view the church is not the kingdom, but it will, through the spread of the gospel, build it. The prefix *post* before millennial means that Christ will come *after* a kingdom has been established. The one thousand years of Revelation 20 or the Millennium are not taken literally.

The Baptist theologian Augustus Hopkins Strong subscribed to postmillennialism and describes it this way:

> Scripture foretells a period called in the language of prophecy "a thousand years" when Satan shall be restrained and the saints shall reign with Christ on the earth. The comparison of the passages bearing on this subject leads us to the conclusion that this millennial blessedness and dominion is prior to the second advent.[1]

Loraine Boettner, a more contemporary postmillennial theologian, defines the system in these words:

> Postmillennialism is that view of last things which holds that the kingdom of God is now being extended in the world through the preaching of the gospel and the sav-

ing work of the Holy Spirit, that the world eventually will
be Christianized, and that the return of Christ will occur
at the close of a long period of righteousness and peace
commonly called *the millennium.* . . . It should be
added that on postmillennial principles the second coming of Christ will be followed immediately by the general
resurrection, the general judgment, and the introduction
of heaven and hell in their fullness.[2]

Actually, evangelical postmillennialism differs from
evangelical amillennialism primarily in its belief in the final triumph of good over evil before Christ returns. Some
postmillennialists believe the entire church or interadvent
age is the Millennium. Others believe the Christianizing of
society will come gradually and be fully realized at a time
in the remote future, but before the return of Christ. For the
postmillennialists, Christ's coming closes this age and is
followed by the eternal state. As we have seen, this is also
believed by amillennialists.

Rise and Development

There were variations in the mid-seventeenth century
as a result of the reaction against humanism and liberal
theology but until the World Wars, postmillennialism was
a most important and influential millennial view. The near
demise of postmillennialism came with the collapse of
utopian dreams in the two World Wars. Today it is a minority view among evangelicals. Another factor in its de-
cline is that postmillennialism found it almost impossible
to stem the tide toward liberal theology. The nonliteral
method of prophetic interpretation that both postmillennialism and amillennialism rest on, leaves the door wide

open, hermeneutically at least, for the same kind of interpretation to be applied to other biblical matters, such as
the deity of Christ, and the authority of the Bible. With
both systems the perplexing question remains: If certain
prophecies can be spiritualized, why not other prophecies
and teachings of the Bible too?

Differences among Postmillennialists

Evangelical postmillennialism as defined above
needs to be distinguished from the liberal theological view
that teaches that a kingdom of God or utopia would be
created on earth through human achievement and better-
ment. The evangelical postmillennial viewpoint is visual-
ized in Chart 14.

Recent Developments

A new kind of postmillennialism different from both
the earlier liberal and evangelical varieties, is gaining popularity and respect today.

The new postmillennialism differs drastically from
the old liberal utopian belief in the future through the suc-
cessful advances of science and technology coupled with
belief in the universal fatherhood of God and brotherhood
of man.

The current expression of postmillennialism is not
exactly like the older variety expressed by evangelicals
such as Augustus Hopkins Strong and Loraine Boettner.
The older view held a special optimism for the final stage
of earth's history and argued for a future utopian age
brought about by the universal spread and acceptance of
the gospel. By contrast, contemporary postmillennialism[3]

believes the kingdom already exists in fulfillment of Old
Testament prophecies and is coexisting with the present
age rather than the special period at the close of the
church age.

The new postmillennialism is aligned closely with
theonomy reconstructionism.[4] The word comes from two
Greek words—θεός. (God) and νόμος (law).

> The word is now being used to designate a new idea
> gaining ground in some circles, particularly those em-
> phasizing Reformed doctrine that the governments of the
> world today should be guided in their judicial decisions
> by all the legislation of the Old Testament and, in partic-
> ular, should assess the Old Testament penalties for any
> infraction of those laws, whether civil or religious.[5]

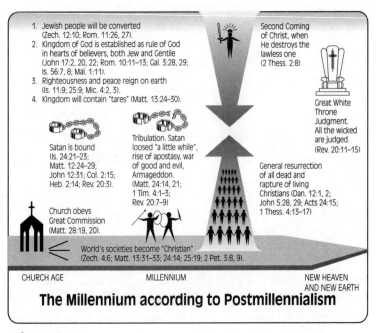

The Millennium according to Postmillennialism

Chart 14

In his book *Theonomy in Christian Ethics,* Greg Bahnsen argues at great length, appealing especially to Matthew 5:17–18, that the Mosaic law constitutes a continuing norm for all mankind. The duty of the civil magistrate is to enforce it—both its precepts and its penalties. "*Every* single stroke of the law must be seen by the Christian as applicable to *this* very age between the advents of Christ."[6] Bahnsen makes no apology in insisting that civil authorities today should be pressured by the church to carry out the death penalty for such things as idolatry, witchcraft, murder, adultery, incorrigibility in children, apostasy, sorcery, false pretensions to prophecy, blasphemy, homosexuality, and sabbath breaking.[7]

Though the new postmillennialism-theonomy package has roots in reformed and amillennial theology, it is being criticized by some in that tradition. Premillennianism rejects it as well.

Summary of the Three Eschatologies

We have set forth the three millennial views and their major variations as held by evangelicals. These were presented in broad outline. The most basic issue that divides the views is the method of hermeneutics or interpretation used when seeking to understand prophecy. The picture is confusing with three different millennial viewpoints and what makes it even more difficult and complex are the variations within each of the millennial views.

Matters can be simplified if we keep some basics in mind: First, with regard to the Millennium, some evangelicals believe the kingdom promises in the Bible have been fulfilled and when Christ returns the eternal state will begin.

Others believe Christ will come again after society has been Christianized. Still others believe the kingdom promises have not been fulfilled but will be when Christ returns and establishes the one thousand-year kingdom on earth before the eternal state begins. In this latter view, the church is in no sense the recipient of promises given to Israel.

Second, with regard to the future seven-year Tribulation, some evangelicals do not believe there is a future seven-year Tribulation at all. For them the Tribulation is now. Among those who do believe in such a time some believe the church will be protected while it goes through the Tribulation. Others believe the entire church will be raptured before any part of the Tribulation begins, while some believe that only spiritual believers will be raptured before the Tribulation starts. Still others hold that the church will experience only the last half of the coming Tribulation.

The question of why these differences over unfulfilled prophecy exist among evangelicals will be explored in Part 3. That the differences are real is no secret, but the reasons they exist are not necessarily widely known.

For Further Thought

1. What distinguishes evangelicals from non-evangelicals when it comes to last days and end-time events?

2. Do you know what millennial system your church subscribes to? What about your best Christian friend?

3. Does a person's view of last days and end-time events make any difference in his lifestyle? Should it?

4. Can you think of any other doctrines of the Christian faith which are affected by one's view of last
days and end-time events?

5. Why do you think Christ's return continues to be
delayed?

🔍 Digging Deeper

Another variation of premillenarianism not included
earlier has been set forth by Robert Gundry in his *The
Church and the Tribulation* (Grand Rapids: Zondervan
Publishing House, 1973). Gundry can be classified not
only as a premillennialist, but also as dispensational in
some respects. Yet he is clearly posttribulational. The publisher predicted that this work would "become the standard text on the posttribulational viewpoint of the rapture
of the church" (from the jacket). This entirely new approach to posttribulationism written from a scholarly perspective remains representative of the viewpoint it presents
and has by no means reached the acceptance expected by
its publisher.

John F. Walvoord, whom Gundry especially cri-
tiqued, responded with *The Blessed Hope and the Tribulation* by the same publishers in 1976. Walvoord shows the
novelty of Gundry's position and how divergent it is from
traditional posttribulationism. Both of these volumes
should be studied to determine their strengths and weaknesses, especially the authors' scriptural defenses.

Other considerable differences exist among evangelical posttribulationists. J. Barton Payne's *Imminent Appearing of Christ* (Grand Rapids: Wm. B. Eerdmans Publishing

Co., 1962) argues for a premillennial posttribulational viewpoint in which the tribulation is spiritualized and imminency is given a new meaning. A comprehensive defense of posttribulationism appears in Alexander Reese's *Approaching Advent of Christ* (London: Marshall, Morgan, and Scott, 1937). He identifies the church as the true Israel that includes the saints of all ages. The church is seen as resurrected at the same time as the resurrection of Revelation 20. Oswald T. Allis argues as an amillenarian for the posttribulational position in his *Prophecy and the Church* (Philadelphia: The Presbyterian and Reformed Publishing Co., 1945).

The Blessed Hope by George Ladd (Grand Rapids: Wm. B. Eerdmans Publishing Co., 1956) represents a futuristic school of interpretation among premillenarians who are posttribulational. He argues that the tribulation is still future but the church will go through it while experiencing God's protection from His wrath.

Ladd also holds that the kingdom promised in 2 Samuel 7 is "now but not yet." He means by this that Christ's presence at the right hand of the Father's throne now is a partial fulfillment of the kingdom promises to David. Ladd's "now but not yet" terminology is also used by those who wish to be called progressive dispensationalists.

6

What Are the Differences?

Christians are at war and the battles are not all being fought against Satan and sin; some of them are being waged against each other. God's people are engaged in a conflict among themselves over their differences about future things. The conflicts cannot always be called "cold wars" either, because sometimes things get very heated.

Why are these disagreements over future events so important? What difference does it make whether a Christian believes, or does not believe, there will be a future earthly kingdom of peace? Is it important to distinguish between the so-called Rapture of the church and the second coming of Christ? Or does it matter all that much? Why is it so important to determine whether Christ, the church, or civil powers establish the kingdom, if in fact it is ever established at all? And if the earthly kingdom of universal peace and righteousness does come, when will it be? The important thing is that Christ will come again to this earth and usher His own into the eternal state, isn't it? What difference does it make whether there is going to be a kingdom on earth or not? To be with Christ is most important and the far better thing after all. Why argue at all for a particular view on the order of things to come since God is sovereign and His plan will be realized and there is nothing we can do about it anyway? In jest, and yet reflecting his desperation, someone described his view of the kingdom and related events as "panmillennialism"—everything will pan out all right in the end. Unfortunately, and needlessly, too many Bible believers share such a view regarding the future.

Let us retrace our steps before we journey any further. We have set forth reasons for another book on prophecy; we do not need another defense of a particular view of the future and certainly not a new view. What we need is a greater knowledge of the divergences that exist and a better understanding among those who hold different viewpoints. Our eyes must look beyond our disagreements over last things to the many things we evangelicals hold in common.

The major events of the future that evangelicals all agree about are presented in the second chapter. In Chapter 3 the different views of the order of future events were given. There we reviewed differences over what will take place when Christ returns and what relation the church will have to any future Great Tribulation.

We come now to that part of our discussion when the reality of the conflict over future events must be set forth. From previous chapters we realize that evangelicals are at odds with each other over God's plan for the future. They are at war over things to come and the battle has been going on for a long, long time, though it has been intensified lately.

A number of things have contributed to this increase in conflict. Perhaps the most significant one has been the recent popularity given the premillennial pretribulational view. This has come through books such as Hal Lindsey's *The Late Great Planet Earth* and Taylor's *The Living Bible.* This is admitted by those who oppose pretribulationism:

> This present popularity of pre-tribulationism is due largely to the widespread use of the Scofield Bible (detailed in the editor's notes) and the many recent authors such as Dwight Pentecost, John Walvoord, E. Schuyler English, and William Pettingill. Many evangelical publishing houses, periodicals, seminaries, Bible schools, faith missions, and popular Bible radio teachers are responsible for its continuing fermentation along with many prophetic films, charts, conferences, gospel songs, and of course recently published paperback books such as *The Late Great Planet Earth.*[1]

Whatever the reason, Christians, members of the same heavenly family, are engaged in a nasty fight with each other over last events and refusing to admit it will not change things. We may not want the people of the world to know about our struggles and conflicts, but they do anyway. Great shame and disgrace has already been brought to the cause of Christ by us over evangelical eschatologies.

The evidence of the fight is overwhelming. I wish I did not have to labor the point, but the purpose in giving these facts is to arouse readers to the reality of the fight so that everyone can be part of easing the tension. The conflict I have exposed here does not thrill me; it saddens me.

Who Started the Fight?

Whoever admits they started a fight? To ask this question of Christians in the struggle over the future is almost like asking two neighborhood boys, "Who started the fight?" that left them both with bloody noses. "He did." "No, he did." The accusations go on and on.

Even if we were certain who started the fight, I am not sure it is worth pursuing. About all it would do is give one side cause for more accusation against the other.

The truth that cannot be denied is, there is a fight. We can call it something nicer if we want to, but that will not change the facts. A difference of opinion is one thing, but an angry warfare involving a bitter suspicious attitude with those who hold a different viewpoint is something else.

The fact is that soon after the apostles passed from the earthly scene, differences developed over end times. The battle has raged among evangelicals at least since the third century. In recent years, the presence of Israel as a nation in the very geographic area promised to her has added fuel to the fire. Premillennialists often point to this phenomenon and say, "I told you so." The amillennialists and postmillennialists respond vigorously, "The nation as a political entity and its presence in the Holy Land has absolutely nothing to do with the fulfillment of prophecy."[2]

Where Is the Battle?

For the most part, theologians, educators, authors, and preachers are the ones wielding the weapons. The people in the pew usually just listen to the viewpoint espoused by the particular person or organization giving information. Of course, it is understandable that a person promote the cause he embraces and thinks is right rather than another one.

So what it amounts to is a fight among the top brass. The evangelical leaders cannot agree among themselves. Conflict does not stop there, though that is where it started. As a result of the popularity of Christianity today, lay people are also becoming involved in the struggle. Families and friends are being divided over differing views of eschatology. The average Christian is reading more than he used to and Christian publishing houses continue to turn out hundreds of books and material on prophecy each year. In fact, some companies that never published books on prophecy before are doing so now. The news media in general includes more information on biblical truth than it did a few years ago. Even bumper stickers now announce the return of Christ.

As a result of the popularity of the teaching of the rapture of the church before the Great Tribulation, the coming man of sin, the world religion and government, the ordinary person is getting a view of the future and sharing it with friends. As a result, differences erupt and the fight of the professionals becomes a fight among the people in the pews as well.

How Goes the Battle?

The furor over the future is a battle of words, but behind the fighting words there are attitudes and feelings that reflect some deep-seated differences.

When strong differences are expressed, each side inevitably accuses the other of being unfair and of misrepresentation. Evangelicals with different views of God's program for the future are no different. It is understandably difficult to present an opposing view as anything less than erroneous when you feel strongly that yours is the true view.

It is understandable that objections will be raised by opposing sides of an issue. Honest differences will always exist as long as there are two people around. But differences and disagreements develop into open warfare when slander of people and views, unsupportable accusations, judgments of motives, name calling, and insinuations are used against those with whom we differ. When this happens, Christian principles are discarded and carnality rules the day. The works of the flesh, not the fruit of the Spirit, are manifest, and honest differences on an issue such as eschatology cannot be expressed without the smell of gunfire and below-the-belt blows. Views of the future program of God are often presented as though those who hold different views could not possibly be evangelical and are less than sincere in their attempts to understand God's Word.

Adherents of each of the views of future events are guilty of unfairness. All the bullets have not been fired from the guns of one particular side. This does not mean that everyone who has ever said anything in defense of his view of things to come has been guilty of staging a war or of fighting unfairly; many disagree without being disagreeable. Unfortunately though, there have been some who have sought to set forth and defend a particular viewpoint by engaging in tactics that have not been fair. Such opponents are certainly not honoring to Christ.

The evidence below reveals the intensity of the fight over things to come from both past and present arguments, and the examples I use are from the anti-premillennial and the premillennial side.

A View from the Anti-premillennial Side

Critics of pretribulationism and dispensationalism have frequently engaged in attacks upon the personalities, the people active in the rise and spread of these points of view.[3] Personal attacks have been used to deter and destroy the positions these people hold.

The guilt-by-association tactic is sometimes used in the discussion of prophecy. One writer drew an analogy between dispensationalism and the destructive higher criticism of the Bible:

> Dispensationalism shares with higher criticism this fundamental error ... despite all their differences, higher criticism and dispensationalism are in this one respect strikingly similar. Higher criticism divides the Scriptures into documents of Scripture which differ from or contradict one another. Dispensationalists divide the Bible up into dispensations which differ from and even contradict one another.[4]

The same writer also implies some relation between Russellism (teaching of the Jehovah's Witnesses) and premillennialism, which have both accepted the Abrahamic covenant as unconditional in nature.[5]

Dispensationalists are said to have "actual contempt for the thinking of historic Christian theology."[6] They engage in "arbitrary and reckless division of the Bible into three compartments."[7] Dispensationalism itself is termed a "heresy" by some nondispensational writers. "Carnal theories" are said to be a part of dispensationalism.

In his classic defense of posttribulationism Alexander Reese leveled his attacks upon pretribulationism with fiery words. One response has caught the tenor of this criticism in these words,

> Mr. Reese does not seem to have made up his mind whether those whom he attacks so tenaciously are fools, or only knaves; his language indeed frequently suggests that they are both! Here are some things he says about them, taken at random as the pages are turned. They are guilty of "aggressive sophistry and fantastic exegesis," and of "paltry reasoning." They prefer "any rubbish to the true and obvious explanation" of a passage and they "wrest the Scriptures." Their preference for the line of teaching they favor is no longer a question of exegesis. . . . They are not God-fearing readers of the Bible but "theorists," "showing little acquaintance with great exegesis." Their teaching is "consistent and ludicrous in its absurdity." "Its effect is to blight 'Bible study' and push their cause all over the world." "It has caused the (Brethren) movement from the beginning." "They wrote their errors on their broad phylacteries. . . ." "They" are "misguided and misleading teachers." And indeed, "Paul informs us that they were *false* teachers who taught thus."[8]

Pretribulationists are said to appeal to "unworthy motives." They want to escape the coming Great Tribulation because they are afraid of it. "Unworthy and selfish impulses" make Christians appeal to the view. Those who believe the church will not go through the coming Tribulation have a strain of "weak-kneed, invertebrate, spineless sentiment."

Premillennialists are said to deal rashly with Scripture. Their position is said to be typical of the wilderness experience of Israel and the amillennial view is typified as the land of Canaan. One passage of Scripture is "superimposed" on another passage. Scripture passages are wedded together in unnatural ways.

Those who subscribe to the premillennial view have a "disease" called "exegetical diplopia, i.e., double vision," in the thinking of one critic. He views the belief of his brethren as "the bifurcated and diplopic premillennial scheme." They are accused of an "artificial interpretation invented to circumvent the clear intent of the passage."

"Pretribulationism is said to have directly and indirectly caused the death of thousands—perhaps millions—of persons." This accusation was made because pretribulationists did not encourage Chinese Christians to leave their country before the communists took over.

Premillennialists and pretribulationists "turn heaven and earth upside down in order to win one convert to their school of thought," and they take the "glory which ought to go to Christ and give it to the nonbelieving nation of Israel."

Dispensationalists have frequently been accused of believing in more than one way of salvation. Though they have cited reasons why they believe in only one way for all time,[9] their opponents still persist in leveling the charge regardless of the evidence to the contrary.[10]

Interpretations given by premillennialists are said to be "symptomatic of dispensationalism's penchant for making unwarranted distinctions and dichotomies." Belief in

national promises yet to be fulfilled in Israel "is a dispensational concoction and is not at all implied in Scripture."

Paul C. Neipp's tract "The Millennium Rapture
Hoax" was written to show that the belief in a Rapture of
the church and the future earthly millennium is a hoax. It
is a doctrine "spun out of thin air." The Rapture theory is
"false" and an "erroneous belief."

"Millennialism is incompatible with the very nature
of faith" wrote one critic. It, in fact, is "dangerous" to the
Christian faith. Another said it is a "fantasy" that even en-
dangers a Christian's salvation. "Millennialism is one of the
anti-scriptural teachings held by a good number of conservatives."

Dispensationalism is sometimes called "an errant
scheme" promoting the desire of things to come "with little desire for the knowledge of holiness."

A View from the Premillennial Side

Is the fight all one-sided? Are the opponents of premillennialism and pretribulationism the only ones who engage in slander and smear attacks? Are they the only ones
really fighting in this battle among evangelicals over things
to come? From the above, the reader may suppose that this
is what I am trying to say, but there is blame on the
doorsteps of premillennialists and pretribulationists as
well. However, since premillennialists have been more on
the offensive than the defensive, it may be that they have
used this method less often.

There is no lack of material written in defense of premillennialism, dispensationalism, or pretribulationism.
However, premillennialism has historically been set forth

as a unified system of theology, which cannot be said for the other views of last things. So the proponents of these beliefs have been mostly involved in attacking the premillennial scheme of events. Jay Adams, an amillennialist, or as he prefers to be called, a "realized millennialist," candidly admitted this of the view he embraces in his book, *The Time Is at Hand:* "Most recent amillennial publications have been largely negative in approach."[11] He also said, amillennialists "have conceived their task as almost fully negative (that is, it consists merely in proving the premillennialist wrong)."[12]

Because they have been primarily involved in attacking the premillennial system, it is understandable that we may find more evidence of this from its opponents. On the other hand, since premillennial pretribulationists have been more engaged in setting forth a positive declaration and defense of their position than they have in opposing their opponent's views, it is only natural to find fewer personal attacks.

This does not mean premillennialists have not made their contribution to the battle; they have. Just as not all who reject premillennial pretribulationism are guilty of the aforementioned charges, so not all proponents are legitimately charged with the following. However, everyone needs to take special precaution to avoid these dangers.

Overstatements of the position, or broad, sweeping, all-inclusive statements that simply cannot be supported, have been made. Premillennial enthusiasts need to be careful about making such generalizations.

This error is perhaps most evident when it comes to hermeneutics. As we have seen, premillennialists propose to follow the literal method of interpretation throughout the Bible. But sometimes when they are saying this and contrasting themselves with amillennialists, premillennialists give the impression that their opponents never employ the literal method and this simply is not true; many of the prophecies of the Bible are interpreted literally by amillenarians. They do not always use the allegorical method. In interpreting most of Scripture, in fact, evangelical amillennialists and postmillennialists use the very same method of interpretation used by the premillennialists. It is only in the understanding of *certain* unfulfilled prophecies that a less than literal approach is followed.

In his defense of amillennialism, William Cox accuses John F. Walvoord, one of the most ardent defenders of premillennialism, of this very thing. He quotes the following from Walvoord, "Premillenarians follow the so-called 'grammatical, historical' literal interpretation while amillenarians use the spiritualizing method."[13] After pointing out that Walvoord later did in fact admit that amillennialists do not interpret *all* Scripture allegorically, Cox accused him of double talk.[14]

There are other areas where premillennialists have overstated their case. It is done sometimes in explaining a passage of Scripture or when referring to those holding variant views. It is easy to say, "Scripture always teaches," or "Nowhere does the Bible say," or "The Church is never called or referred to as. . . ." The same tendency to overstate applies to references to individuals too. Statements such as, "all amillennialists" or "all posttribulationalists," or "no amillennialist or posttribulationalist ever . . ." are much too sweeping.

The guilt-by-association technique has also sometimes been used by premillennialists. This usually comes up when the important subject of hermeneutics is discussed.

It is a fact that there are few, if any, theologically liberal premillenarians because premillennialists follow the literal method of interpreting all the Bible. It is also true that theological liberals and Roman Catholics embrace amillennialism. The same method used by evangelical amillennialists in interpreting certain prophetic Scripture is freely used by theological liberals and Roman Catholics. It is true, the literal method, when consistently used, is a great obstacle to liberal theology and Roman Catholic theology,[15] but by no means are all who do not literally interpret Scripture thereby liberal or Roman Catholic.

Guilt by association is also often applied when peculiarities of a particular person are attributed to all who share his basic view. There are, as we have noted, significant variations within amillennialism, postmillennialism, and posttribulationalism, but an alleged error or overstatement by one person must not be charged to all in his eschatological camp. Neither should a minority view be attributed to the majority as is sometimes done.

There have also been times when premillennialists have left vague and false insinuations by the way they have presented their case. Sometimes what is left unsaid is more damaging than what is said.

I think it would be very easy to get the impression from some premillennial and pretribulational writing that those not holding that position are really less than honest. Impressions of dishonesty and purposeful misrepresentations are sometimes created by the way things are presented.

The way some premillennial pretribulationalists state and explain their positions, it would be easy to believe anyone who disagrees with them could not possibly be evangelical. I have taught in the college and seminary classroom for over thirty-five years and have found that my students are often shocked to learn that there are amillennialists and postmillennialists who are thoroughly evangelical. They sometimes do not get that from things they hear and read, and their lack of knowledge adds fuel to the fire of opposition in the long run. Some of the greatest Bible commentaries, devotional books, and theology books have been, and still are, authored by those who are not premillennial or pretribulational. Amillennialists as well as postmillennialists have been, and are, among the stalwarts of the historic Christian faith. Great men of God do not all accept the same view of things to come.

Not a few pretribulationists give the impression they have all the answers to the problems of the future. An attitude of pride often comes through in what they say and write and they give the impression that their view has no problems. Some are even bold to make pronouncements in areas where angels fear to tread. For example, Israel's existence as a nation on May 14, 1948, and her occupancy of the city of Jerusalem in 1967, have resulted in unnecessary dogmatism about the future of the nation.[16] On what scriptural ground, for example, can it be dogmatically affirmed that this is the "terminal generation"?

One frequently hears or reads the premillennial pretribulation view expressed as though the opposition were biblical imbeciles. Statements like these give this impression: "Even a cursory reading of the passage. . . ." "The simple reading of the passage makes this meaning apparent." "Dedicated students of the Bible know. . . ." "The premillennial view is clearly taught throughout Scripture. . . ."

I do not want to judge the motives of anyone engaged in the struggle described above. Many times those who make strong statements against their opponents or in defense of their own position do not mean them as they are understood. But whether or not unchristian attitudes exist or harm is intended, what is said often does grave injury to others and to the cause of Christ. Therefore, great care must be exercised when our viewpoints are expressed lest our differences degenerate into bitter, all-out warfare.

There is simply no place in the family of God for name-calling, false accusation, slander, evil insinuations, and the guilt-by-association technique. God forgive us all of such sins.

For Further Thought

1. When did you first learn about the evangelical differences concerning end-time events?
2. Are evangelical differences concerning end-time events very pronounced where you live? Why do you think this is so?
3. Does anything else characterize those who hold to a particular view of future events?
4. Do you think any of the charges and counter-charges you read about in this chapter are true? What percentage of them?

5. Why do you think it would not be wise to stop all preaching and teaching about end-time events in an effort to stop the war?

Digging Deeper

Within premillennial dispensationalism there is what some in the movement call developing dispensationalism, and others, who are not happy with the development call, departing dispensationalism. In other words, some see what is happening as a healthy sign of development, of progress. Others, however, fear the mood reflects a serious departure from the very foundations of dispensational theology and is likely to result in the demise of dispensationalism for many, especially those pursuing the new trends and their followers.

What is the primary area of development that is causing so much stir? It is over the relation of the present church age to the Davidic Covenant or, in other words, the relation of the church to the messianic kingdom. The conflict is not new.

Premillennialists who have been posttribulational have always advocated the "already, not yet" of Christ's kingdom. They frequently referred to the present and future aspects of Christ's kingdom. See for example, George Ladd's *The Presence of the Future* (Grand Rapids: Wm. B. Eerdmans Publishing Co., 1974).

Today, however, there are those who claim to be premillennial, dispensational, and pretribulational who believe that some form of the messianic kingdom is present now. This is a new development. They argue that while there will be a future one-thousand-year reign of Christ, His messianic kingdom was instituted in some form or sense when He was here. For further study of this viewpoint see Robert L. Saucy, "The Presence of the Kingdom and the Life of the Church," in *Bibliotheca Sacra* (January/March 1988) 145:33, and an unpublished paper, "The Reign of the Lord Jesus Christ" a post Evangelical Theological Society copy (December 1987; address request to the author Darrell Bock, Dallas Theological Seminary, 3909 Swiss Avenue, Dallas, Texas, 75204). For a defense of the more traditional view see H. Wayne House and Thomas Ice, *Dominion Theology: Blessing or Curse?* (Portland, OR: Multnomah, 1988) 217-48; and also Alva J. McClain, *The Greatness of the Kingdom* (Winona Lake, IN: BMH Books, 1959).

Three books have been published recently defending the traditional view that the Davidic kingdom will only begin when Christ returns with His saints. These reaffirm normative dispensationalism while critiquing progressive dispensationalism. J. Dwight Pentecost in *Thy Kingdom Come* (Wheaton, IL: Victor Books, 1990) argues that the future one-thousand-year reign of Christ on the earth is a part of God's whole theocratic kingdom. It is God's final demonstration of His right to rule on the earth. The church will rule and reign with Christ in that earthly kingdom, but the messianic kingdom is in no sense present today. The kingdom believing sinners enter when they trust Christ is the kingdom of God's dear Son (Col. 1:13), but this is not the kingdom associated with the Davidic Covenant of 2 Samuel 7.

Renald E. Showers in *There Really Is a Difference!* (Bellmawr, NJ: The Friends of Israel Gospel Ministry, Inc.,

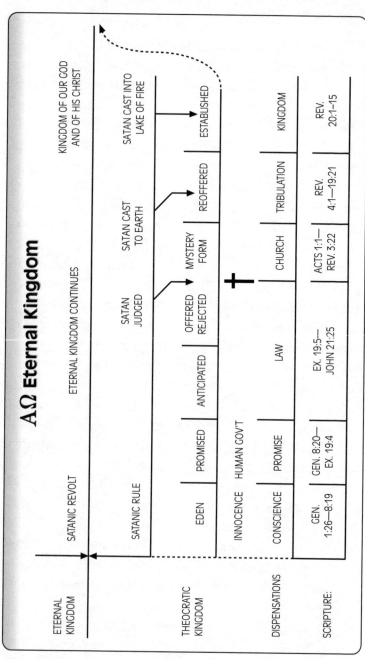

Chart 15

1990) argues cogently for the contrast between covenant theology and dispensational theology.

Charles C. Ryrie has revised and enlarged his *Dispensationalism Today* under the title *Dispensationalism.* The new work interacts at all crucial points with progressive dispensationalism.

The "already, not yet" teaching regarding the messianic kingdom is also embraced by contemporary postmillennial reconstructionists. David Chilton, for example, said, "The kingdom was established when Christ came. But it has not yet reached its full development" (*Paradise Restored* [Tyler Reconstruction Press, 1958], 73-74).

Chart 15 illustrates how normative historical premillennial dispensationalism views the future messianic kingdom in relation to the larger theocratic or meditorial kingdom program of God. It does not see the Messiah's kingdom operative in any sense today.

Part 3

WHY THE VARIANT VIEWS OF THINGS TO COME?

7

Interpreting Scripture

Though they all embrace its inspiration and authority, evangelicals who defend a particular view of events to come do not all understand Scripture in the same way. They understand it differently because they use different methods of interpreting some of the unfulfilled prophecies of Scripture. This is the most basic reason for the differences over *pre-, a-,* and *post*millennialism. It also has much to do with the differences over the relation of the church to the coming Great Tribulation.

The science and art of biblical interpretation is called "hermeneutics," and it is easy to see that a method of interpretation, a system of hermeneutics, is most important to the understanding of God's Word.[1] Without it, the Bible is a closed book, which is true of all literature. Whenever we read anything, we unconsciously follow certain rules of interpretation so that we may understand the material. What does this mean? is the question every reader often asks without even thinking about it.

The interpretation of Scripture is one of several crucial matters related to the total doctrine of Scripture. A brief review of these related matters will help us put things in focus before we discuss the bearing that interpretation has upon the differences over things to come.

The meaning of the interpretation of Scripture is related to the revelation, inspiration, authority, canonicity, and illumination of the same Scriptures. Chart 16 illustrates the order and relation of these aspects of Scripture to each other and emphasizes the divine and human elements in each.

Interpreting Scripture

REVELATION HEBREWS 1:1	GOD REVEALING, HUMANITY LISTENING
INSPIRATION 2 TIMOTHY 3:16	GOD CONTROLLING, HUMANITY RECORDING
AUTHORITY JOHN 10:35	GOD ENFORCING, HUMANITY OBEYING
CANONICITY JUDE 1:3	GOD PRESERVING, HUMANITY RECOGNIZING
ILLUMINATION 1 CORINTHIANS 2:10–12	GOD CLARIFYING, HUMANITY UNDERSTANDING
INTERPRETATION 1 CORINTHIANS 2:12	GOD ENABLING, HUMANITY DECLARING

Chart 16

Revelation, in reference to Scripture, means the act of God whereby He made Himself and His will known to man. God gave the revelation; man received it. God has revealed His Word to many human penmen over about 1,500 years of time. The earliest and simplest revelation is just as true, just as inspired, as the later revelation. It is the amount of information about Himself and about all He has made known which has progressed. Therefore, in order to know what God has said about Himself, or any subject, the whole needs to be examined. The later revelation never changes or corrects the earlier recipients or locations as, for example, from Israel to Israel and the church or from earth to earth and heaven.

Inspiration has to do with the recording of the revelation. When we speak of the inspiration of the Bible like Paul did in 2 Timothy 3:16–17, we are referring to God's work of guiding and controlling the human writers of Scripture in the very choice of the words used in the original manuscripts. The result of this divine work upon the fallible, human writer was the recording of God's message without error or omission in all its parts.

Because the revelation recorded without error in the Bible came from God, it is of course divinely authoritative. It bears the very *authority* of the One who gave it.

The God who gave His Word also preserved it for us. From the very time the revelation was given and recorded it was accepted by God's people as His Word. We call the human recognition of God's Word by His people the *canonization* of Scripture.

The Holy Spirit, who was used in the giving, receiving, and acknowledging of God's Word, is the one who enables the child of God to understand it. This we call the *illumination* of Scripture.

My purpose in presenting this brief background in the doctrine of Scripture has been to distinguish the science of biblical interpretation from the other facets of the doctrine and to show its relation to them. Historically, evangelicals have had little difference over the revelation, inspiration, authority, canonicity, and illumination of Scripture,[2] but they have not ever agreed on a method of interpretation to be followed uniformly throughout the Bible. Nor is there agreement on how the doctrine of progressive revelation affects one's hermeneutics. There is also considerable difference among evangelicals over the relation of the Old Testament to the New and how the use of the Old in the New relates to the question of biblical interpretation.[3]

Is there a single method of interpretation to be used throughout Scripture, or do some parts of the Bible require a different method? How does the way the New Testament uses the Old affect one's eschatology, his view of things to come? Such issues greatly divide evangelicals and the result is much fighting.

Importance of the Issue

When it comes to the understanding of prophecy or events to come, the most important question is: How is it to be interpreted? What does this prophetic Scripture mean? Representative spokesmen of each of the various evangelical views of things to come candidly admit that indeed this is the important issue. All must agree—although some are more reluctant to admit it than others—

that they disagree about events to come because they interpret the prophecies differently.

Here are a few admissions which illustrate my point.

Oswald T. Allis put the issue bluntly. His book, *Prophecy and the Church,* was intended to show what he felt was error in premillennial dispensationalism and to defend his own view of amillennialism. He said:

> Old Testament prophecies if literally interpreted cannot be regarded as having been yet fulfilled or as being capable of fulfillment in the present age. It is consequently assumed by premillennialists that they will be so fulfilled during the Millennium when Satan will be bound and the saints will reign with Christ.[4]

A more contemporary amillennial writer reflected the same view in these words:

> One very basic conflict between different millennial groups is their hermeneutics—the manner in which they interpret the Bible. In fact, this difference is what divides equally conservative men into different camps with reference to the Millennium. This fact is acknowledged frequently by all millennial schools of thought. Each of the millennial views has been held by conservative, scholarly men who were devoted to the correct interpretation of the Bible and all have looked on the Scriptures as being divinely inspired and as the Christian's only rule of faith and life.[5]

In his recent book, *The Time Is at Hand,* Jay Adams also revealed the importance of the interpretation of unfulfilled prophecy:

> In this transition from pre to posttribulationalism, some have gone further and are beginning to test the founda-

tions of premillennialism itself. In the process, doubts about fundamental presuppositions have arisen. Having rejected the unbiblical principle of exclusively literal interpretation of Old Testament prophecy, many no longer look upon the so-called "nation Israel" as God's chosen people. They cannot agree to a "Jewish millennium" fully equipped with rebuilt Temple and restored sacrificial system. They find no indication of a utopian-type millennium anywhere upon the pages of the New Testament.[6]

Loraine Boettner, evangelical postmillennial theologian, expressed his awareness of the crucial importance of one's method of interpretation. He agrees the basic reason for different views of things to come has to do with principles of biblical interpretation:

> That believing Christians through the ages using the same Bible and acknowledging it to be authoritative, have arrived at quite different conclusions appears to be due to different methods of interpretation. Premillennialists place strong emphasis on literal interpretation and pride themselves on taking Scripture just as it is written. Post and amillennialists, on the other hand, mindful of the fact that much of both the Old and New Testament unquestionably is given in figurative or symbolic language have no objection on principle against figurative interpretation and readily accept that if the evidence indicates that it is preferable.[7]

But amillennialists and postmillennialists are not alone in acknowledging the importance of biblical interpretation for the understanding of things to come; premillennialists also agree wholeheartedly. Their writings on the future are filled with emphatic statements on this point.

The Theocratic Kingdom of Our Lord Jesus the Christ is a classic three-volume set in defense of premillennialism. In it, George N. H. Peters states his view of the importance of a proper method of interpretation:

> The literal, grammatical interpretation of the Scriptures must (connected with the figurative topical [sic] or rhetorical) be absorbed in order to attain a correct understanding of this kingdom. Its import is of such weight and the consequences of its adoption of such moment, the tendency it possesses of leading to the truth and the vindicating Scriptures of such value that we cannot pass it by without some explanations and reflections.[8]

A contemporary spokesman for premillennialism voiced the same understanding of the importance of the interpretation of prophecy:

> There is a growing realization in the theological world that the crux of the Millennial issue is the question of method of interpreting Scripture. Premillenarians follow the so-called "grammatical historical" literal interpretation while amilleniarians use a spiritualizing method.[9]

It is an accepted fact; nobody debates the issue. The method of interpretation one uses is crucial to the understanding of what is read. This is no less true of prophetic Scripture than of any other literature.

The Methods of Interpretation

Two methods of interpreting the Bible are prominent today. Other methods have been suggested in the history of the church[10] but the literal, or normal, and the spiritualizing, or allegorical method, have been and still are the two most prominent and important methods.

The Literal or Normal Method

Premillennial Christians usually pride themselves in their belief in the literal interpretation of all of the Scripture. They are frequently described by friends and foes as "literalists." They are sometimes called "wooden literalists," which implies they do not allow for types and symbols in their understanding of Scripture. That criticism does not seem to square, however, with the fact that premillennial writers have contributed much to the understanding of these areas of biblical study.

By a literal interpretation of Scripture, premillennialists mean a straight interpretation. To them, the Bible is to be interpreted just like all other literature. "The literal interpretation as applied to any document is that view which adopts as the sense of a sentence, the meaning of that sentence in usual, or normal conversation or writing."[11] "To interpret literally means nothing more or less than to interpret in terms of normal usual designation."[12]

Premillennialists are agreed in accepting the above as an accurate definition and description of their method of interpreting the whole Bible.

The literal method of interpreting Scripture is also called the grammatical-historical method. This designation emphasizes that the meaning of Scripture is determined both by the grammatical and the historical considerations.

Premillennialists, especially dispensational premillennialists, have not failed to support their use of the literal, normal, or grammatical-historical interpretation of Scripture. Many reasons are often given by them in defense of their position,[13] but there seem to be three crucial reasons:

Philosophically, the purpose of language itself seems to require literal interpretation. Language was given by God for the purpose of being able to communicate with man. . . . If God be the originator of language and if the chief purpose of originating it was to convey His message to man, then it must follow that He, being all wise and all loving, originated sufficient language to convey all that was in His heart to tell men. . . . The second reason why dispensationalists believe in the literal principle is a Biblical one. It is simply this: The prophecies of the Old Testament concerning the first coming of Christ—His birth, His rearing, His ministry, His death, resurrection—were *all* fulfilled literally. There is no nonliteral fulfillment of these prophecies in the New Testament. . . . A third reason is a logical one. If one does not use the plain, normal, or literal method of interpretation, all objectivity is lost. What check would there be in the variety of interpretations which man's imagination could produce if there was not an objective standard which the literal principle provides?[14]

Premillennialists insist the New Testament's use of the Old Testament substantiates the literal method. In support of this, reference is often made to the many Old Testament prophecies that were fulfilled literally in the New Testament. Why, premillennialists argue, should we expect unfulfilled prophecies to be fulfilled any differently?

Appeal is also made to Jesus' method of interpreting the Old Testament. It seems clear from His example that He used a normal, literal, historical-grammatical method. His interpretation of Scripture was always in harmony with the grammatical and historical meaning. Jesus frequently interpreted one passage of Scripture by appealing to another passage to add further clarification to the meaning (i.e., Matt. 19:3–8 and Deut. 24:1; cf. Matt. 12:3–7 and Hosea 6:6).

The Spiritualizing or Allegorizing Method

According to proponents of this view it is simply impossible to apply the literal method of interpretation to all of Scripture. Amillennialists and postmillennialists insist on this and, especially in prophetic portions, employ a less than literal method at times.

Oswald T. Allis, for example, believes a thoroughly literal interpretation of Scripture is impossible.[15] He gives three reasons for his belief:

> (1) The language of the Bible often contains figures of speech. This is especially true of its poetry. . . . (2) The great theme of the Bible is God and His redemptive dealing with mankind. God is a spirit; the most precious teachings of the Bible are spiritual and these spiritual and heavenly realities are often set forth under the form of earthly objects and human relationships. . . . We should remember the saying of the apostle that spiritual things are "spiritually discerned". . . . (3) The fact that the Old Testament is both preliminary and preparatory to the New Testament is too obvious to require proof.[16]

Premillennialists have not failed to respond to these objections.[17]

No matter which view one takes, however, it must be admitted that not until the third century A.D. and the Alexandrian school of theology was there any serious opposition to the literal method. Teachers in this school—Clement of Alexandria and Origen—used a method of interpretation that made all Scripture an allegory. In the fifth century, Augustine led a rejection of this movement. He did not completely reject the allegorical method, but taught that only prophecy needs to be allegorized or spiritualized. Much of biblical truth was salvaged by Augustine's efforts. Yet, he and many of his followers, including the great Reformers, continued to use the allegorical method in their interpretation of some unfulfilled prophecy.

Luther, Calvin, and others of the Reformers stressed the need for the literal sense of Scripture and a grammatical-historical approach and they stressed the literal meanings in arriving at their view of salvation by faith alone and the inspiration and sole authority of the Bible. But they did not apply those principles to their interpretation of *all* unfulfilled prophecy.

In addition, those who reject the spiritualizing approach argue further that the spiritualizing or allegorizing method of biblical interpretation did not arise out of a desire to understand Scripture. Instead, it owes its birth to heathen philosophy. "The allegorical system that arose among the pagan Greeks was copied by the Alexandrian Jews and was next adopted by the Christian church, and dominated the church to the Reformation."[18] The allegorical or spiritualizing method of interpretation may be defined as "the method of interpreting the literary text that regards the literal sense as the vehicle for a secondary, more spiritual and more profound sense."[19]

Premillennialists believe such a method for seeking to understand the meaning of any part of Scripture has very serious dangers. They question such a method: What is the basic authority in interpretation—the Scriptures or the mind of the interpreter? They do not feel that the allegorical method really involves interpretation of Scripture. How can the conclusions of the interpreter who uses this method be tested?

Do not all evangelical expositors of the Bible use the literal, historical-grammatical method? Could anybody possibly be evangelical if he did not apply this method to the biblical teaching about Christ, salvation, and sin? These are questions literalists ask of allegoricalists. They believe evangelicalism results only by following the literal method. Premillennialists are convinced that the system of hermeneutics they use is a tremendous safeguard against liberal theology.

All evangelicals do use the literal method for their understanding of most of the Bible, but some, namely those of amillennial and postmillennial persuasion, think it best to use a less than literal hermeneutic with much unfulfilled prophecy. It is at this point that the evangelical world is divided over things to come and this is what puts prophecy in the middle of the debate. Premillennialists cannot understand why their Christian brothers and sisters insist on using a different method in interpretation with some unfulfilled prophecy but not with all of it. They wonder on what grounds is the less-than-literal approach to be restricted to only some themes of unfulfilled prophecy?

To summarize the differences between the two schools of thought, this may be said. All evangelicals use the literal method in their interpretation of the Bible. Some evangelicals believe this same method is to be used with *all* Scripture; these are the premillennialists. Other evangelicals believe that while the literal method is to be used of Scripture in general, it is not necessarily to be used with all unfulfilled prophetic portions. Some of the biblical prophecies (i.e., those concerning the first advent of Christ) are to be understood literally and in fact were fulfilled literally,[20] but many prophecies related to the future coming again of Christ must be understood in a less-than-literal way.

8

The Methods of Interpretation and the Covenants

God made some staggering promises to His people, His chosen representatives. These promises are presented to us in the form of covenants. Evangelical Christians all agree with this. What they do not all agree on is the nature and meaning of these covenants. How are they to be understood? To whom specifically were they given? Are they conditional, depending on man's obedience for their fulfillment, or are they unconditional, depending solely upon the "I will" of God for their fulfillment? To a large extent the way such questions are answered determines one's view of things to come.

There are four basic covenants in the Old Testament that especially relate to things to come. In truth, it is not too much to say that one's view of these covenants determines his view of things to come. In each of these covenants, God promised specific things to the people of Israel, His own people.

The Four Biblical Covenants

The Four Biblical Covenants diagram (p. 103) shows the importance of the Abrahamic covenant and the relation of the other three to it. The features of the Abrahamic covenant—land, seed, blessings—are each developed further in the later covenants.

What, in fact, did God promise in these biblical covenants? Let us examine each of them to see what they include without respect to a particular view of events to come. Before we do that, we should define a biblical covenant. The word *covenant* appears frequently in the Bible. Relationships between God and man, between men, and even between nations are referred to as covenants. As used in the Bible, a covenant is a contract or an agreement. Some of the covenants in Scripture are obviously conditional—the stated conditions must be met by both parties involved. Other covenants do not stress conditions and seem to be unconditional in nature. They appear, therefore, to depend only upon the truthfulness of the one who proposes and makes the covenant for their fulfillment. In the four covenants we will study now, God Himself made the covenants.

The Abrahamic Covenant

Now the Lord said to Abraham, go forth from your country, and from your relatives and from your father's house, to the land which I will show you; And I will make you a great nation, And I will bless you, and make your name great; and so you shall be a blessing; And I will bless those who bless you. And the one who curses you I will curse. And in you all the families of the earth shall be blessed (Gen. 12:1–3).

Confirmation and enlargement of this great covenant is recorded in several other Scriptures (Gen. 12:6, 7; 13:14–17; 15:1–21; 17:1–14; 22:15–18; Ps. 69).

A reading of Genesis 12:1–3 reveals that some of the promises of God to Abraham were personal. Some were concerned with the nation that would come from his loins, but others were universal.

God promised to bless Abraham by giving him a great name, making him a channel of blessing to others, dealing with others as they dealt with him and his seed, and giving him an heir by Sarah (Gen. 12:1–3; 15:4). These promises all concerned Abraham as an individual.

A great nation was to be born from Abraham's seed (Gen. 12:2, cf. 17:6). This nation was promised the land of Canaan as an everlasting inheritance (cf. Gen. 17:8). God also promised that the covenant would be established with Abraham's seed and it would be "everlasting" (Gen. 17:7).

God said to Abraham, "In you all the families of the earth shall be blessed," (Gen. 12:3). This obviously reaches beyond Abraham and even beyond his physical seed. This aspect of the covenant is generally referred to as universal.

The burning questions are: Have any of these promises to Abraham, the father of the Jewish race, ever been fulfilled? Has fulfillment of all of them occurred? If any have been fulfilled, which ones are they and how were they fulfilled? What about the remaining promises? Does the nation Israel really have a future in God's program? The answer to these and other similar questions has great bearing upon one's view of things to come. As soon as we ask questions like these we are touching upon the crucial differences among evangelicals over events to come.

The Palestinian Covenant

This covenant is called Palestinian because it concerns the land of Palestine. At the end of Moses' leadership, when Joshua was about to begin his work, the people of Israel were still not in possession of the land God had promised them. They were at the entrance of it, but not in it. To complicate things further, there were enemies in the land. Was the land of Palestine really going to be the possession of the people of Israel? Was God going to fulfill His promise in spite of all their unbelief and in spite of the enemies' opposition?

God's answer to these questions came in the form of a covenant:

Now it shall come to pass, when all these things come upon you, the blessing and the curse which I have set before you, and you call them to mind among all the nations where the LORD your God drives you, and you return to the LORD your God and obey His voice, according to all that I command you today, you and your children, with all your heart and with all your soul, that the LORD your God will bring you back from captivity, and have compassion on you, and gather you again from all the nations where the LORD your God has scattered you. If any of you are driven out to the farthest parts under heaven, from there the LORD your God will gather you, and from there He will bring you. Then the LORD your God will bring you to the land which your fathers possessed, and you shall possess it. He will prosper you and multiply you more than your fathers. And the LORD your God will circumcise your heart and the heart of your descendants, to love the LORD your God with all your heart and with all your soul, that you may live. Also the LORD your God will put all these curses on your enemies and on those who hate you, who persecuted you. And you will again obey the voice of the LORD and do all His commandments which I command you today. The LORD your God will make you abound in all the work of your hand, in the fruit of your body, in the increase of your livestock, and in the produce of your land for good. For the LORD will again rejoice over you for good as He rejoiced over your fathers, if you obey the voice of the LORD your God, to keep His commandments and His statutes which are written in this Book of the Law, and if you turn *to* the LORD your God with all your heart and with all your soul (Deut. 30: 1–10).

There are several tremendous promises enumerated in this covenant: Because of unfaithfulness, the nation would be taken from the land (verses 1–3 cf. Deut. 28:63–68); Israel's Messiah would return (verses 3–6); Israel would be restored to the land (v. 5); As a nation, Israel would be judged (v. 7); Full blessing from God would come to the nation Israel in God's time (v. 9). These are things the text clearly states. The question is, how are they to be interpreted? What do they mean?

At a later time in Israel's history this covenant was confirmed by God Himself (Ezek. 16:1–7); Apparently it had not yet been all fulfilled by the time of Ezekiel's writing (592–570 B.C.). Has the covenant ever been fulfilled completely? Has the nation Israel ever possessed *all* the land promised her by God in this covenant? Christians differ in their answer to such questions but their replies explain the fight about things to come; they understand the biblical covenants differently.

The Davidic Covenant

To David, God said:

> When your days are fulfilled and you rest with your fa-
> thers, I will set up your seed after you, who will come
> from your body and I will establish his kingdom. He
> shall build a house for My name, and I will establish the
> throne of his kingdom forever. I will be his father and he
> shall be My son. If he commits iniquity, I will chasten
> him with the rod of men and with the blows of the sons
> of men. But My mercy shall not depart from him, as I
> took it from Saul, whom I removed from before you. And
> your house and your kingdom shall be established for-
> ever before you. Your throne shall be established forever
> (2 Sam. 7:12–16).

These words came from God to David after he had
expressed his desire to build a temple for the Lord. David
wanted to replace the temporary portable tabernacle with
a beautiful and permanent temple for the worship of God.
His intentions and ambitions were certainly commendable
even though God did not permit him to fulfill them. The
covenant is confirmed by God in Psalm 89, which means
that it had apparently not yet been fulfilled by that time.

Three specific promises from God to David stand out
in this covenant: He would have a son, a posterity, called
in the covenant his "seed"; the "throne" of David was to
be established forever; and, the "kingdom" of David was
also to be established forever.

Three things were also promised to Solomon,
David's son, in the covenant. He would be the one to
build the temple that David had aspired to build.
Solomon's throne, God promised, would also be estab-

lished forever. The chastening hand of God, the covenant said, would come because of disobedience, yet the covenant would be fulfilled.

Again the question must be asked: Has this covenant ever been fulfilled? If it has, how and in what sense has it been fulfilled? If it has not, will it ever be realized, and if so, how will this become a reality? Christians are divided over their answers to these questions.[1]

There is one more biblical covenant that closely relates to things to come and needs to be considered.

The New Covenant

All who believe the Bible to be God's Word agree that God promised Israel a new covenant when He said to and through the prophet Jeremiah:

> Behold, the days are coming, says the LORD, when I will make a new covenant with the house of Israel and with the house of Judah—not according to the covenant that I made with their fathers in the day that I took them by the hand to lead them out of the land of Egypt, My covenant which they broke, though I was a husband to them, says the LORD. But this is the covenant that I will make with the house of Israel after those days, says the LORD: I will put My law in their minds, and write it on their hearts; and I will be their God, and they shall be My people. No more shall every man teach his neighbor, and every man his brother, saying, "Know the LORD," for they all shall know Me, from the least of them to the greatest of them, says the LORD. For I will forgive their iniquity, and their sin I will remember no more (Jer. 31:31–34).

Most important of all, the new covenant assures Israel of a new heart. The promise was that God's law will be written in the hearts of the people (v. 33). Iniquity will be removed from the people and their sin will be remembered no more: (v. 34). The Holy Spirit of God, it is promised, will teach and find the people's hearts obedient and responsive (v. 34). Great material blessing will accompany Israel when she is brought into the land (Jer. 32:41). Hosea also speaks of an unprecedented outpouring of the favor and blessing of God upon the people of Israel (Hos. 2:19–20).

Several questions confront the student of Scripture as he seeks to understand this covenant. To whom was the covenant given in the first place? Was it a conditional or an unconditional covenant? Has it ever been fulfilled? Is it being fulfilled at the present time or does it await fulfillment in the future? How are we to understand the references to the New Covenant in the New Testament? These questions are answered differently by evangelicals.

There are three views among premillennialists as far as the interpretation of this covenant is concerned. One view is that there are really two covenants—one for Israel and one for the church. Another view is that the New Covenant is Israel's and it has no relationship to the church. The third and most popular view is that there is only one New Covenant but it has two aspects—one applies to Israel and the other applies to the church. It is the death of Christ that provides the basis for both aspects.

Two Views of Covenants

Premillennialists argue strongly that each of these four biblical covenants is unconditional; that is, they believe the fulfillment of the covenants does not depend upon man's response but rather solely upon God. This does not mean, of course, that man's behavior in response to God and His covenants is not important. It means that while man's obedience or disobedience affects his relation to the blessings of the covenants, his disobedience does not nullify or make void what God has promised. God will do what He has promised. He will see to it that His Word is carried out, the premillennialists argue.

Staunch defenders of the premillennial system speak at length of the unconditional nature of these covenants. John F. Walvoord argues that all of Israel's covenants were unconditional with the exception of the Mosaic covenant:

> The Abrahamic Covenant is expressly declared to be eternal and therefore unconditional in numerous passages (Gen. 17:7, 13, 19; 1 Chron. 16:17; Psa. 105:10). The Palestinian Covenant is likewise declared to be everlasting (Ezek. 16:60). The Davidic Covenant is described in the same terms (2 Sam. 7:13, 16, 19; 1 Chron. 17:12; 22:10; Isa. 55:3; Ezek. 37:25). The New Covenant with Israel is also eternal (Isa. 61:8; Jer. 32:40; 50:5; Heb. 13:20).[2]

Altogether Walvoord presents ten reasons for believing in the unconditional nature of the Abrahamic covenant.[3]

Lewis Sperry Chafer, founder and first president of Dallas Theological Seminary and well known for his premillennialism, was very vocal in his belief that four biblical covenants were unconditional. Of the Palestinian covenant in particular, he said,

> What is usually termed the Palestinian covenant is the oft-repeated declaration by Jehovah, wholly uncondi-

tional, that the land which was promised to Abraham—
"to your descendants have I given this land from the
river of Egypt unto the great river, the river Euphrates"
(Gen. 15:18)—would be Abraham's possession forever. It
is thus deeded to Abraham personally and becomes the
legal inheritance of his posterity. On what other ground
could it be styled "the promised land"?[4]

J. Dwight Pentecost, an articulate spokesman for premillennialism, argues similarly for the unconditional nature of the Davidic covenant. He insists that it is called an
eternal covenant (2 Sam. 7:13) and therefore must rest for
its fulfillments upon the faithfulness of God. Since the Davidic covenant is primarily an expansion of the "seed" portion of the Abrahamic covenant, it must be unconditional
and partake of the same character as the original
covenant. And furthermore, Pentecost argues, the reaffir-
mation of the Davidic covenant after repeated acts of disobedience by Israel proves beyond any question its unconditional nature.[5]

Charles C. Ryrie, another champion of the premillennial cause, also argues that all four of the biblical
covenants are unconditional in nature. Of the New
Covenant he said,

> The New Covenant is an unconditional, grace covenant
> resting on the "I will" of God. The frequency of the use
> of the phrase in Jeremiah 31:31–34 is striking (cf. Ezek.
> 16:26–62). The New Covenant is an everlasting
> covenant. This is closely related to the fact that it is un-
> conditional and made in grace.[6]

In addition to believing that the biblical covenants
are all unconditional, premillennialists also believe they

were originally given to the people of Israel and *not* to the church. Furthermore, they insist, the national promises embodied in these covenants will therefore be realized by the nation to whom they were given and not by the church. The national Jewish promises have not been, nor will they ever be, transferred to the church.[7]

Ryrie is representative of normative premillennialism and is a recognized spokesman. Concerning the Abrahamic covenant he said,

> Does the Abrahamic Covenant promise Israel a permanent existence as a nation? If it does, then the church is not fulfilling Israel's promises, but rather Israel as a nation has a future yet in prospect; and does the Abrahamic Covenant promise Israel permanent possession of the promised land? If it does, then Israel must yet come into possession of that land for she has never fully possessed it in her history.[8]

Later he says, "Israel means Israel and her promises have not been fulfilled by the church. Since they have not, they must be fulfilled in the millennium if God's Word is not to be broken."[9]

We now have a better understanding of what premillennialists believe about the four biblical covenants related to last events. But what do amillennialists and postmillennialists believe about these major biblical covenants?

The classic and contemporary amillennial understanding of the covenants sees all of them as either conditional in nature and thus abrogated because of Israel's disobedience, or as transferred to a "spiritual Israel," the church. Oswald T. Allis, a leading exponent of amillennialism, cites six reasons for believing the Abrahamic covenant was conditional: (1) a condition may be involved without being stated; (2) obedience is always a precondition of blessing; (3) the sign of circumcision proves there was a condition; (4) being in the land was a precondition of blessing; (5) Esau had to be restored for full blessing under the covenant; and (6) certainly the fulfillment of the covenant depends upon obedience to Christ.[10]

Amillennialists disagree among themselves about the biblical covenants. Many contend that the covenants were conditional, and the people to whom they were made did not meet the conditions. Therefore the conditions, and thus the covenant promises, were not and need not be fulfilled. Yet a significant number of amillennialists argue that the promises of the covenant were fulfilled historically in the Solomonic reign. Still others insist the promises are being fulfilled now by the church.

William Cox, a contemporary convert from premillennialism to amillennial thinking, said this about the Abrahamic covenant:

> Since the covenant was conditional, the contract is broken and God is not bound to Israel as a nation. His covenant now is with the faithful remnant and with the Gentile believers. These two groups constitute the Christian church which today is the Israel of God (Gal. 6:16).[11]

Of the new covenant, he also said,

> Though the covenant was made with Judah and Israel of the Old Testament, it was fulfilled in the spiritual Israel of the New Testament, that is, the church. Even this, however, was prophesied in Scripture such as Zechariah 2:11. (Compare also Romans 15:8–12.)[12]

Louis A. DeCaro differs slightly with the traditional amillennial approach to the Abrahamic covenant. He said:

> The promise of land in the Abrahamic Covenant was historically fulfilled. That Israel lost it through disobedience is not chargeable to God. He gave ample warning through His servants, the prophets, that Israel would be dispossessed of the land if persistent in disobedience. The restoration after the Babylonian captivity served the climatic purpose of the covenant—to bring Christ into the world. Since then, there is no more need for territoriality in the plan of God. There remains no more territorial fulfillment. The promise of the seed found its immediate fulfillment in Old Testament Israel, the nation through which Jesus Christ came into the world. Christ, with the ultimate in the seed of Abraham, is the mediator of the covenant blessing. The proliferation of the seed continues in those who are united with Christ through faith in Him. In respect to Israel today there is no national purpose remaining in the covenant which directly relates to the divine program of redemption. The claim of Israel today to Palestinian soil has no covenantal basis. The *de facto* existence of Israel today in Palestine today is simply a secular Zionist attempt to fuse Judaism with statecraft. It is highly questionable whether this fusion of Judaism with statehood is related to either covenantal or prophetic thought.[13]

The postmillennial interpreters present a somewhat different view of the biblical covenants from that expressed in the amillennial system, though by no means agreeing with their premillennial brethren.

For example, Loraine Boettner, champion of the postmillennial faith, made this observation in his presentation and explanation of Scripture setting forth the new covenant:

These are very great and precious promises and certainly they point forward to conditions that have not yet been enjoyed on this earth. They are, in fact, so far-reaching and expansive that they stagger the imagination. Some amillennialists finding no place in their system for these conditions attempt to carry them over into the eternal state. But references to the "nations" (Isa. 2:2, 4); judging the people with righteousness (Isa. 65:20); etc., point unmistakably to this world.[14]

While in this way expressing his dissatisfaction with the amillennial interpretation of the covenants Boettner also revealed the same dissatisfaction with premillennial views:

The promise given to Abraham that his seed should be very numerous and that through his seed all the nations of the earth should be blessed, finds its primary fulfillment not in the totality of his physical descendants as at first sight would seem to have been indicated, nor even in the descendants through Jacob who stood in a special relationship to God, but in those who are his spiritual descendants (Gal. 3:7, 29); and the seed through which all the nations of the earth were to be blessed was not his descendants in general, but one individual, which is Christ.[15]

The postmillennial view of the thousand years of Revelation 20 and the possibility of Christ's literal reign from the throne of David reveals how the biblical covenants are viewed. As expressed by J. Marcellus Kik:

The term thousand years is a figurative expression used to describe the period of the Messianic Kingdom upon earth. It is that period from the first advent of Christ until His second coming. It is the total or complete period of Christ's kingdom upon earth.[16]

Kik continues,

> As a matter of fact, there is not one text in the New Testament that speaks of Christ literally reigning upon earth in the literal city of Jerusalem. That is a teaching which is prevalent in some circles, but it is not taught by Christ or the apostles.[17]

Charles Hodge, a postmillennial theologian of years gone by, expressed a similiar view of the biblical covenants. In his presentation of arguments against the restoration of the Jews to the Holy Land, he said:

> The idea that the Jews are to be restored to their own land and there constitute a distinct nation in the Christian church is inconsistent, not only with the distinct assertions of the Scriptures, but also with its plainest and most important doctrines.[18]

A contemporary postmillennial writer expressed his view of the biblical covenants as he set forth his mandate for the church:

> Christianity is destined to take over all the kingdoms of the earth. God has given His people a "covenant grant, to take possession and exercise dominion over His creation. . . . The church is to take the initiative in fighting against the forces of evil—she must attack, and not merely defend—and she will be successful. She must pray for, expect, and rejoice in her enemies' defeat. God will give His Church enough time to accomplish her assignment.[19]

There are two reasons why so much attention has been given to the biblical covenants. First, these covenants are absolutely essential to one's view of future events. No student of Scripture who wishes to learn about end-time events can avoid them; they must be taken into account in deciding what things are yet to come. Second, and as a result of their importance to future things and their extensive revelation in the Bible, the covenants are a source of major difference among Christians. Christians get involved in combat over events to come because they disagree on the meanings of the biblical covenants, and this is because they follow different methods of interpretation as we have seen earlier.

Evangelicals all agree that the fulfillment of prophecies provides strong evidence for the inspiration and authority of the Bible, but they are unable to agree on if or how the prophecies have been fulfilled. Premillennial Christians go one step further and say the way in which prophecies have been fulfilled literally gives the believer warrant for saying the unfulfilled ones will, indeed, be fulfilled in the same way—literally.

For Further Thought

1. What is the result of interpreting Scripture dealing with the Christian faith allegorically rather than literally?

2. How does the interpretation of Scripture relate to the other areas of the doctrine of Scripture?

3. Do those who say they interpret Scripture literally ever use any other method of interpretation? When and why? What about those who interpret it allegorically?

4. Why do some evangelicals base their view of

   end-time events on the biblical covenants and
   others do not?

5. Which of the biblical covenants is most important
   to end-time events? Why?

 Digging Deeper

Hermeneutics, the science of biblical interpretation,
lays the foundation for the exegesis of the Bible. Everyone
who seeks to understand the Bible follows certain principles of interpretation whether they are conscious of it or
not. Charles C. Ryrie lists four different hermeneutical systems or methods of interpreting Scripture *(Basic Theology*
[Wheaton, IL; Victor Books, 1987], 110–13). He calls these
four the allegorical, the literal, the semiallegorical or semi-
literal, and the theological. Ryrie believes the correct system is the literal, which he prefers to call the normal or
plain.

   Premillennial pretribulational dispensationalists insist
that they use this method consistently throughout Scripture. They contend also that many other evangelicals use
the same method in order to determine and defend all the
cardinal doctrines of the faith, but when it comes to some
specific aspects of eschatology, however, they feel that
many of these same evangelicals use a less than literal
method.

   A survey of amillennial and postmillennial writings
does seem to demonstrate a less than literal approach to
the interpretations of eschatological passages and portions
of books such as Revelation. Defenders of these systems
either insist this is not the case, or agree it is and then seek

to justify it. For an illustration of this see Oswald T. Allis, *Prophecy and the Church* (Philadelphia: The Presbyterian and Reformed Publishing Co., 1947). Reading James Montgomery Boice's chapter, "How to interpret the Bible" in his *Foundations of the Christian Faith* (Downers Grove, IL: InterVarsity Press, 1986), one would expect him to be a dispensationalist, but he is not. His outlined principles of interpreting Scripture seem to be identical with dispensationalists, however.

Some contemporary dispensationalists are raising questions about just how consistently their peers do use the literal method of interpretation. They are not altogether sure a consistently literal hermeneutic is in fact an aspect of the *sine qua non* of dispensationalism as Ryrie claimed in his *Dispensationalism Today* (Chicago: Moody Press, 1965). See the following for examples: Robert L. Saucy, "The Critical Issue between Dispensational and Non-Dispensational Systems," *Criswell Theological Review* (1986), 154–55; Robert L. Saucy, "Contemporary Dispensational Thought," *Tyndale Student Fellowship Bulletin* (March–April 1984), 6–7; Kenneth L. Barker, "False Dichotomies between the Testaments," *Journal of the Evangelical Theological Society* 25 (March 1982); and Craig A. Blaising, "Development of Dispensationalism by Contemporary Dispensationalists," *Bibliotheca Sacra* 145 (July–September 1988), 254–80.

9

Why the Differences Persist

As noted in the previous chapter, the debates that theologians, educators, and preachers have over the order of future events have filtered down to the lay people. On the professional level, there is conflict over events to come because of hermeneutics, the method of interpreting the Bible, but on the nonprofessional level, there are many more reasons why the fighting continues.

Levels of Differences

These two levels are not altogether isolated from each other, of course. Many times those we refer to as professionals are tenacious in their beliefs for the very same reason the nonprofessionals are. So, while certain unfulfilled prophecy has, in fact, been put in the ring by the professionals, the people at ringside watching the fight have also gotten involved. So even though the question of how to interpret Scripture is very basic to the conflict, there are also many other reasons for the fighting.

The purpose of this chapter is to name some of these additional reasons and to discuss them briefly. Some are more important than others but all are a part of the reason why evangelicals seem to be at swords' length over unfulfilled prophecy.

Conflict has been going on for a long time with neither side willing to concede much. When those in the ring are too weak to keep fighting, they are quickly replaced by others who carry on the struggle, and some of these contestants are not very Christian in their behavior. Sometimes you would hardly know that another member of the body of Christ was being discussed.

The real issues are not clear. You may wonder if these people are really being honest, but when you talk about the different viewpoints with others in the grandstand, you soon find yourself taking sides. Before you know it, you are arguing with your best friend. Bad feelings develop and soon you find yourself with a circle of friends who share your views, or at least most of them.

Reasons Why Differences Persist

Hermeneutics, as has been noted, is without question the most basic reason for the fight over prophecy, but there are other reasons. Without any particular importance in the order in which these are listed, here are some additional things that keep the conflict raging.

Traditionalism

None of the major creeds of the church include premillennialism, amillennialism, or postmillennialism in their statements. Those who place much emphasis upon church creeds in traditional beliefs find it difficult to embrace a view not included in the beliefs of the ancients. That is understandable.

The danger to be avoided here is that of equating the creed or traditional belief with the Bible. The question is, does the creed indeed restate what the Bible teaches? Only the Bible is inspired of God and therefore divinely authoritative. In the final analysis, Scripture must be our first and most basic creed.

In the history of biblical doctrine, eschatology was last on the list for discussion. The ancient church fathers first studied and formulated doctrinal statements on the doctrines of Scripture, God the Father, God the Son, God the Holy Spirit, sin, salvation, and the church. Only after the Reformation was there any lengthy and specific concentration on future events. So one looks in vain for definitive statements regarding any of the various systems of eschatology in the doctrinal formulations of the ancient ecumenical councils of the church. The person and work of Christ were the chief concerns of the early church fathers, not a well-defined order of events in connection with His second coming.

One difference over unfullfilled prophecies is that some Christians place more emphasis and importance upon ancient beliefs and creedal statements than others do.

Relation to Other Truths

Serious students of Scripture know that the way they understand God's plan and program for the future bears upon a number of related matters in God's Word. Other biblical teaching relates directly to the doctrine of last things. For example, one's view of unfulfilled prophecy, to be consistent, will determine one's view of certain things about the church and Israel and vice versa. Much of the

Old and the New Testament will be understood differently according to the particular view of future events one embraces.

Because these relationships between biblical truths exist, it is very natural for people to be reluctant to change and give up a certain view of events to come to replace it with another view. If they do, it means other areas of doctrine need to be restudied and readjusted too.

Even present daily Christian life is affected by one's understanding of God's calendar of future events. Arthur D. Katterjohn, who believes the church will go through the coming Great Tribulation, highlighted the importance of future things to present Christian experiences:

> Does the church of today face the intensifying of sin and lawlessness resulting ultimately in the revelation of sin (Antichrist) and his persecution of the church to a degree never before experienced, before we are gathered together unto Jesus Christ at His return? Or . . . are we to look for the Rapture—that secret and imminent catching away of the church to heaven before that time of tribulation? Your answer to the above question has a great bearing upon your activities as a Christian in the next few years. If the first alternative is indeed correct, then we must teach that the church is to prepare for that great persecution, making haste in the light of the present-day fulfillment of prophecies and the increasing decadence of mankind and his way of life.[1]

Current World Events

The crisis times in which we live draw attention to what the Bible has to say about the future. As man's attention is drawn to the unfulfilled prophecies of Scripture and he learns of various views of those prophecies, sides will naturally be taken and tensions will mount.

In 1948 the state of Israel was formed. In 1967 during the Six Day War, Israel occupied all of the city of Jerusalem. Russia and China have become world powers. The world is threatened by famine. World powers have it in their hands to destroy each other. The 1988–90 European move toward unification must also be taken into account. We could go on and on naming things that have made men's hearts fail them for fear. Even the present evident failure of atheistic Communist governments brings great fear and uncertainty.

Because of what is going on in the world, the Christian public, and even many of the unsaved, are beginning to turn to the Bible for answers. They find that much of what is taking place in the world seems to parallel predictions of Scripture. Then they discover the differences that prevail over exactly what the Bible teaches about the future. While God's Word is clear in its teaching about certain crucial events in the future, it is not always as clear in the specifics and the order in which the events will unfold. In other words, there are areas of prophecy that are not spelled out in a particular passage, leaving room for different interpretations. Various passages and issues must be brought together. Pieces of the eschatological puzzle must be put in place, but not all Christians see the pieces in the same way. Some of the pieces appear to fit in more than one place, and some of the pieces are often forced and made to fit even though they really do not. Thus the conflict continues.

Stubbornness

Nobody will want to admit that he just may have in him a streak of what was called "bullheadedness" when I was a boy. Today, we say a person with those same characteristics is opinionated. Now a certain amount of that kind of thing, when properly distributed, has its place. But when we refuse to even hear the other side or admit areas of weakness in our own position, we have put on the boxing gloves. We have stepped inside the ring and what is more, we have probably made up our minds to stay there as long as we live, and indeed, to win the fight.

A number of reasons for this unchristian attitude could be cited. Maybe we are stubborn—like we are in other areas of our lives too. If things are not the same way we think they should be, do we think they are all wrong? Are we going to change our ideas or our ways when it is obvious that a change is for the better?

Prejudice

Sometimes we are so prejudiced we can't look at our view objectively. By and large people believe what they have been taught. There are exceptions, of course, but usually what we have been taught, and what we have read, conditions us so that we embrace those views with few modifications. Then after we have believed those things, shared them with others, and perhaps identified ourselves with the view and those who hold it, change does not come easy. Who of us enjoys admitting he has been wrong?

And, therefore, the fight goes on. All too often no

one or no amount of information will make us change our view. Isn't that really about the way it is? It is unfortunate that we are that way, but we are. It simply is a rather common attitude among people—even Christian people.

Insufficient Information

Admitting a lack of sufficient information is difficult for some to acknowledge. Not necessarily through any fault of their own, large numbers of lay people have only a sparse knowledge of why they and their church or pastor hold certain beliefs. Generally speaking, people leave doctrinal beliefs up to the clergy. If they like a church and/or have been reared in it, they give general consent to its teaching, especially in areas of future events and accept them without question. Generally speaking, lay people do not bother to examine the theological beliefs of their church either before they join or afterward.

It would be interesting to ask an average group of Christian people from a variety of churches what they themselves believe about the future and why. Much of the hassle over God's future program for the world and many a round in the fight might be eliminated if Christians would really seek to understand why they hold certain beliefs. If we don't think we have the time or the interest to study our beliefs, then at least we should be less dogmatic in holding them and less judgmental and condemnatory of those with differing viewpoints.

Selfishness

Can we face the thought that it is not unusual for some to promote a certain view because it gives them the image of a leader? They enjoy holding a view that is some-what unique, and, naturally, there are always numbers of people who will be followers. Such people seem to enjoy rabble-rousing when they and their cause become popular.

Such a spirit is often also associated with an attitude of dogmatism. Certain personalities seem to have that kind of bent to them, feeling they must be right about every-thing. They cannot tolerate any ambiguity, uncertainty, or unanswered questions. Everything is always either black or white, yes or no. There is never any place for the gray, the uncertain.

Spiritual Pride

Whenever we feel we have a corner on God's truth we give evidence of spiritual pride. It is foolish to think we have all the answers or that our view is free of all prob-lems; yet we often become selfish and proud in our view of what God is going to do in the future and our knowl-edge of it. We often fight with other members of the family of God because we are sinfully selfish and proud.

Escapist Mentality

After talking to a number of people over a number of years I have come to believe that many believe the church will be delivered from the future seven-year Tribulation simply because they can't imagine enduring the horrors of it. They basically don't believe they will go through it sim-ply because they want to escape it. They don't want to be in it, and there are few who wouldn't want to escape it. Yet, it must be realized that some saints of God will be in that awful time of unprecedented trouble. In fact, the Bible says a large number of them will be.

Martyr Complex

Strong feelings of desire to be absent during the future outpouring of God's wrath lead to quarrels with those who don't believe the church will escape that awful time but will somehow be protected through it.

The martyr complex is another thing that keeps the fighting going. While some Christians wilt when they think of the future Tribulation, others—often with pride—say they will be happy to suffer for Christ through that time. After all, history records that many of the martyrs in days gone by had the same attitude. Often those who boast of willingness to die for Christ look askance upon those who want to be delivered from the coming Great Tribulation. Both of these attitudes continue to divide the body of Christ.

Overstatements and Misrepresentations

It is not hard to find broad, sweeping statements that have caused division. Just start with the professionals who represent all the various views of things to come. One's zeal and enthusiasm must be harnessed so that they do not lead to erroneous statements.

When the professionals are guilty of overstatements and misrepresentations, it is not surprising to find the same coming from the laity. Though they do not intend to misrepresent, that is often exactly what results. Many times what is claimed for a particular view is really not true to the facts. Half-truths, unwarranted dogmatism, and incomplete presentations only add fuel to a fire that is already too hot and has been burning entirely too long.

Honest Exegetical Problems

If the Bible were as clear in its teaching of the details and order of events for the future as it is on what a man must do to be born again, there would be less room for different views on the subject. But God in His wisdom has not seen fit to present all truth in the same way and to the same extent. He has chosen to give us some things in broad outline, with less emphasis upon the specific details. We need to respect the silence of God as much as we do His spoken word.

We are responsible, though, for all of God's truth when it speaks on matters essential to the faith, such as the deity of Christ, His vicarious atonement, man's total inability to merit favor with God, and the total authority of Scripture. Evangelicals do not differ on these matters but there is room for difference over how some of the unfulfilled prophecies will be fulfilled. This is true simply because there are passages of Scripture which when taken by themselves may be legitimately used for differing points of view.[2] All the scriptural evidence is not on the side of any one particular viewpoint.

Semantics

Merriam-Webster's *New Collegiate Dictionary* defines *semantics* as "the study of meanings."

I believe the fighting over the future keeps going on partly because not everybody means the same thing by the words they use. Terms like *kingdom, Second Coming, re-*

turn of the Lord, dispensation, and literal mean different things to different people. These need to be defined and understood clearly. If they are not, needless conflicts will arise. We must not be quick to assume what is meant when words with different usages and meanings are used interchangeably and synonymously.

Straw Men

By "straw men," I mean a view not literally held by the one to whom it is assigned. Literature in defense of the various evangelical views of future things frequently include straw men. A certain belief is said to be held by those who embrace a particular view of the return of the Lord and accompanying events. Sometimes a belief is terribly misstated. But when these "straw men" appear in print or are preached from pulpits or taught in classrooms, they are soon so closely associated with the view that they become genuine bones of contention among God's people.

There are doubtlessly other things that serve to continue the fighting about the future. The ones listed above have come to my attention as I have examined my own heart and head, the literature from all sides, and am constantly involved in a cross-section of evangelicals.

What can we do to change the situation? We can personally withdraw from the battle. We can and should take a long hard look at ourselves and our attitudes. Are we disagreeing with our brothers and sisters in Christ in the spirit of Christian love and respect for them? Does genuine honesty mark our response to God's Word and His people? Is our particular view based upon what we really believe that the Bible teaches or is it just "party-line" we are promoting? We need to do our best to be a part of the solution and not a part of the problem as we talk about things to come.

For Further Thought

1. Why do you hold certain beliefs about events surrounding the return of Christ?
2. Have you always believed as you now do? If you have changed, why?
3. If you believed Christ could return at any moment, how would it affect your life?
4. Do you recognize any areas of your thinking about God's plan for the future that need changing?
5. If there are areas that need changing, how do you plan to make the changes?

🔍 Digging Deeper

Sometimes individuals who embrace a particular view of end-time events embarrass others who hold the same view and they even put the view in poor light by their radical and extreme viewpoints.

This has happened through the years and continues to go on among those who believe Christ will return literally. I refer particularly to date-setting for Christ's return. The Christian and non-Christian world's attention has been drawn to this recently with the publication and distribution (300,000 claimed) of Edgar C. Whisenant's *88 Reasons Why the Rapture Could Be in 1988* (Nashville, TN: World Bible Society, 1988) and his *On Borrowed Time*. I recommend Manfred E. Kober's *How Soon the Rapture?* (Ankeny, IA: Faith Baptist Bible College, 1989) for an exposé and refutation of Whisenant's work.

Date-setting for end-time events is of course not new. The founder of Adventism, William Miller, predicted Christ would return in 1843. Taze Russell of the Jehovah's Witnesses set 1914 as the date of Christ's return. Herbert W. Armstrong, and his son, Garner Ted Armstrong, said in 1966 the kingdom of Christ would come in ten or fifteen years.

Hal Lindsey, who rather recently popularized the pretribulational view, predicted Christ would return about forty years after the May 14, 1948 establishment of the nation Israel. See his *The Late Great Planet Earth,* and his more recent: *The 1980's: Countdown to Armageddon,* in which he asserts that this present generation is the one that will witness the return of Christ.

Edgar C. Whisenant's prediction referred to above was accompanied with considerable boasting that he had incontrovertible proof that his date for Christ's return in 1988 was correct and, only if the Bible was wrong, could he be wrong. When it became obvious he *was* wrong, he changed the date to January 1989 and later updated it again to September 1989. Such dogmatic error serves only to hurt the cause with which it is associated.

Gary North, for example, in his foreword to Greg L. Bahnsen and Kenneth L. Gentry, Jr.'s book, *House Divided* (Tyler, TX: Institute for Christian Economics, 1989), uses Whisenant's behavior as normative and descriptive of dispensationalism (xxii). North's vitriolic approach to brethren with whom he differs is reflected in the "P.S." he added at the end of his foreword to the book: "Neither Dr. Bahnsen nor Dr. Gentry is responsible for my 'unchristian, offensive, insensitive, uncharitable, confrontational, argumentative, arrogant, unscholarly style,' as it has been described on occasion. They are both certified for seminary employment. As for me, I prefer off-campus bonfires" (xivi).

Such behavior among God's people can only serve to further divide evangelicals on end-time events. It accomplishes nothing good and only does great harm. One more example of the same is to be found in Dave MacPherson's *The Late Great Pre-Trib Rapture* (Kansas City, MO: Heart of America Bible Society, 1974). In this little paperback the author ridicules those who hold the pretribulational viewpoint and makes numbers of unfounded charges.

Part 4

WHAT CAN I DO?

10

Steps Toward a Solution

There is no question about it—prophecy is in the ring—to use the language of the sport of boxing. The ancient bout has been, and still is, with fellow believers, and it has resulted in a lot of bloody noses, black eyes, and even some broken bones. Serious injury and sometimes almost irreparable harm has been done to the body of Christ as a result of the conflict. Some of God's people seem to keep their gloves on all the time. Always on the alert, they wait for every possible opportunity to fight another round in the ring. Sometimes they make the opportunity if none seems to be forthcoming.

I would like to sincerely and seriously plead with my fellow evangelicals to join me in taking prophecy out of the boxing ring. The fight has accomplished little for good. I can't believe God has been or is pleased with the fight.

Suggestions for Solutions

The following suggestions are made in connection with my appeal.

Have Convictions

When I suggest we take prophecy out of the ring, I do not mean Christians should not have firm beliefs about future events. On the contrary, I believe strongly that God's people ought to have convictions regarding future things. This applies both to professionals and nonprofessionals. What one believes about unfulfilled prophecy is very important. I have not been saying that everything other than belief in the Second Coming, the future Resurrection, judgment, and eternity is peripheral. Everything in God's Word is crucial; nothing is insignificant with God.

As a part of Christian growth and maturity, every believer ought to grapple with what the Bible teaches, including what it teaches about the future. Honest effort should be put forth to correlate Scripture and to see that it all fits into a pattern. Everything in God's Word is important and that includes unfulfilled prophecy, all of it. It is highly important that we understand as best as we can what lies in store for us as individuals, the church, and the world in general. After all, God has spoken on the subject; He has told us what He wants us to know.

A lot of unfulfilled prophecies of future events are very clear in Scripture. As we have seen, evangelicals all agree on these because there is little room for difference. But what should we do about those areas where evangelicals do not agree? Unfortunately far too many have thrown up their hands in despair and said, "It's all a mystery. We can't know anything for sure about the future." No good can ever be accomplished by such an attitude. Such neglect of divine teaching cannot be pleasing to the Lord either.

I suggest we take it as a challenge to study the Bible

carefully and seek to understand as the Holy Spirit teaches us what God wants us to know about the future. No book of the Bible is a closed book. Some have felt this way about the books of Daniel and Revelation, which is unfortunate. God gave His Word to us so that we might know Him, His will, and His ways. He wants us to understand His Word, otherwise there would have been little point in giving it to us and preserving it for us.

The Holy Spirit is the divine teacher of every child of God. He, Christ promised, will lead His own into all truth (John 16:13-14). Each believer has received God's Holy Spirit so that he might "know the things that have been freely given to us by God" (1 Cor. 2:12). He teaches us however from the written Word of God. As we prayerfully study the Scriptures, therefore, the Spirit will take what God has revealed and make it real to us. All who have been born again "have an anointing from the Holy One" (1 John 2:20). The "anointing" of the Spirit is the portion of every child of God (1 John 2:27).

God has gifted men and women and has given them to the church. We should avail ourselves of the fruit of their labors. There are many books available that present the various views of unfulfilled prophecy. After God's Word has been studied, it will be helpful to see how others understand it and used it, or even misused it, in their system. A bibliography of select volumes briefly annotated has been included in this book to assist your understanding of the various views from those who embrace them.

Hold Convictions in Love

We can be sure God has a plan that will be carried out in the fulfillment of prophecy. He wants His people to believe and study His Word—all of it—so they will know what it teaches and fashion their lives accordingly. What one believes about future events matters and it matters much because other truths are affected by that belief. It is right to have and to hold definite beliefs about the future.

What is wrong, and what unfortunately seems to be rather prevalent, is the affirmation of our views in ways which are not Christ-like. We may be one hundred percent correct in what we believe, but if we do not hold those views in humility and with genuine Christian love for other believers who differ from us, we have sinned. It is not always easy, but our goal should always be to speak the truth as we understand it in love (Eph. 4:15).

Evangelicals believe the whole Bible. They believe everything it teaches to be true. And, yet having said that, in all honesty we must add that there are some things in Scripture that we hold with more certainty than other things. For example, we can be altogether certain the Bible teaches that Jesus Christ will come again to this earth, but we might not be nearly as certain about the identity of the twenty-four elders of Revelation 4:4 or of the man of sin in 2 Thessalonians 2:3. This being the case, let us display more humility, patience, and tolerance toward others and their viewpoints in these areas where Scripture is not clear or definite. Let's hold our views and share our differences as fellow members of the family of God. Let's not suspect people of being less than orthodox just because they don't subscribe to the viewpoint on prophecy that we have been taught and believe and that may, or may not, be the true view.

It is not wrong for churches, schools, and other organizations to have clearly stated specific views regarding the future. In fact, it is a strength. These institutions have a right to expect those associated with them to hold the same views. Nor should there be a halt of prophecy conferences and publication of books and other literature in defense of particular views of events to come.

By no means do I hope for, nor am I calling for, a scrapping of all attempts to outline the order of events in the future. Scripture does go beyond the general teachings of Christ's second coming, future resurrection, judgment, and eternity to come. There are a significantly large number of passages that must be harmonized, related, and reconciled with those broad teachings. It is the believer's responsibility to rightly divide the Word of truth, and that, of course, includes prophetic truth (2 Tim. 2:15).

The church has always grown and prospered more through proliferation than it has through attempts at external unity:

> The creative forces of the Christian faith have been unleashed not by unity but by proliferation. . . . Unity is, in fact, not a healthy tradition for religious faith. . . . The great spiritual movements of mankind have not been uniting movements but proliferating movements. Proliferation is the sign of life and health.[1]

The words above were written in response to the modern liberal attempt to build a world church but they are also applicable to the issues discussed in this book. The need is not for all views of eschatology to somehow be amalgamated into one broad, all-inclusive belief. The differences need not be damaging; they can provide stimulation and vigor, provided that those who hold them do so in a God-honoring way.

I am calling for an honest attempt to be more Christian over our differences. Let us speak the truth, but let's be sure it is the truth. Then let's be doubly sure we speak in love, that fruit of the Spirit that is love.

Scripture does tell us to fight, but not over prophecy. Paul told Timothy to fight the good fight of the faith (1 Tim. 6:12), and it is a responsibility that every believer has. However, the specifics of unfulfilled prophecy can hardly be called essentials of the faith once delivered to the saints. We, like Timothy, are all to keep the faith (2 Tim. 4:7), but "the faith" surely cannot be construed to mean a particular order of future events. Yes, we are to do battle for God with the armor He provides (Eph. 6:13-18), but the battle is to be against sin, Satan, and all the forces of evil.

Evangelicals have so much in common. It is a shame that we so often fight each other instead of our real enemies. Some seem more willing to oppose and attack a brother who has a slightly different view of things to come than they are those who deny the faith (2 Pet. 2:1; 2 Cor. 11:13-15).

They are often more willing to join hands for some Christian cause with those who deny the faith than they are with other evangelicals who are not aligned with their view of future things.

There are those evangelicals who believe, as long as one holds to their particular view of eschatology, all other doctrinal matters will somehow be in line. Their particular kind of eschatology has almost been made a cure-all for other ills and a preventative from all future departure from the faith. History simply does not substantiate such thinking.

Evangelicals who have strong convictions about things to come desperately need to keep their views in proper perspective, and I number myself among them. We need to exert ourselves against the real enemy of our souls and of the faith once delivered to the saints. God give us courage to have and to hold convictions concerning the future. May He also give us humility, patience, and love toward those who have not seen the light as we have.

Suggestions for Action

Perhaps we could learn from how children in rural Japan are said to meet their difficulties. This could be very helpful for evangelicals with differing views of unfulfilled prophecy.

It might be called pillow education. Whenever a child has a difficulty or difference with another child, he sits on one side of a pillow. His hands are placed on it and he says, "I am all right and my friend is all right." Then he moves to another side of the pillow, places his hands on it and says, "My friend is right and I am wrong." Next he moves to the third side, places his hands on the pillow and says, "Both my friend and I are wrong and both of us are right." Finally the child moves to the fourth side of the pillow, places his hands on it and, often in deep thought, says, "I am partly right and my friend is partly right."

All the positions that evangelicals hold on unfulfilled prophecy have strengths and weaknesses. No one view is all right and all the others all wrong. As we allow the Holy Spirit to teach us through the Word, we must embrace the view that we feel is taught in Scripture and has the fewest and least bothersome problems.

What practical things can be done about the fight over the future? Are there any definite steps we can take to help eliminate the fighting? I believe there are. It will do little good to read a book like this and be reminded of the facts of the fight unless we are motivated to take definite action toward removing the unnecessary friction and easing the tension. These things apply to professionals and nonprofessionals alike.

Take Positive Action

There are certain positive actions that all of us as adult Christians can and should take if we are determined to help ease the tension over future events:

1. Determine to understand opposing views better and why they are held.
2. Determine to be less caustic about other evangelicals and their views of future events.
3. Determine not to suspect a person's orthodoxy because he doesn't agree with you.
4. Determine to cooperate and build fellowship whenever and wherever possible with those evangelicals who hold different views of unfulfilled prophecy.

Some Negative Action Needed

Some negative action can also go a long way toward bringing about positive results:

1. Avoid majoring on minors.
2. Avoid unwanted dogmatism and conclusions.
3. Avoid a holier-than-thou attitude.

4. Avoid giving the impression that you have all the answers and others have all the problems.

5. Avoid thinking a view must be without problems or it can't be right.

An epithet appears in a Latin treatise designed to uphold Lutheranism and at the same time call for peace in that church. This treatise reportedly was published in Germany sometime between 1615 and 1630. The message of the poem is most fitting for our day as well, especially in regard to differences over God's plan for the future. I can't think of a better suggestion for action than this. Translated into English it reads:

> In essentials, unity.
> In uncertainties, freedom.
> In all things, love.

For Further Thought

1. Do you have strong convictions about end-time events? Which events and why?

2. How do you feel toward those who differ with your views?

3. In what areas could there be more cooperation among evangelicals with differing views of eschatology?

4. How can you be an agent for healing between those at odds over unfulfilled prophecy?

5. What specific steps do you intend to take to be that healing agent?

11

Be Ready: The New Millennium and the Second Coming of Christ

There is no question about it, the Bible predicts a number of things about mankind's last days on earth. Christians may not agree on how to interpret these prophecies, but there can be no doubt that the Bible records them.

As we have seen in this survey of last days, the Bible is more specific and clear about some future events than it is about others. That Jesus promised He would come to earth again, that the dead would be raised and judged, and that there is a heaven to gain and a hell to shun cannot be denied by those who believe the Bible.

The question is, How shall we then live?

The world is about to embark on the year 2000; a new millennium is just around the corner. Is that date significant to biblical prophecy? Every day we are moving closer to Christ's return. Does what the Bible says about these major end-time events make any difference to you? So what? That is the question many are asking.

The Bible anticipates both a one-world church and a

one-world government in the last days. There are certainly signs and forerunners of both in the news today. According to the Bible, both will be in existence before Christ returns and rights all wrongs and brings perfect peace and justice to the world.

The New Millennium

Several years ago, anticipating the year 2000, *Time* and CNN conducted a telephone poll of eight hundred adult Americans, asking them what they thought life would be like in the next millennium. The questions covered a broad area of topics such as religion, communication, political leadership, and economics. Here are four of the questions asked and the answers given. These reveal current thought about the anticipated new millennium.

Q. Compared with the twentieth century, do you think the twenty-first century will have more:

> Wars—32 percent
> Environmental disasters—59 percent
> Poverty—61 percent
> Disease—53 percent
> Hope for the future—62 percent

Q. Do you think the world will be in better shape at the end of the twenty-first century than it is today?

> Better—41 percent
> Worse—32 percent
> About the same—15 percent

Q. Will religion play a greater role in the lives of people in this country after the year 2000?

> Greater—55 percent
> Lesser—27 percent

Q. Will the second coming of Jesus Christ occur some-time in the next one thousand years?

Yes—53 percent

No—31 percent

The only way for us to know what we may expect as the year 2000 and beyond approaches is to know first of all at least the major end-time events predicted in the Bible. This book has highlighted these and the ways evangelicals believe they will unfold.

Once we are clear on what the Bible teaches in these areas we are in a position to interpret historical happenings and current events accordingly. At all cost we must avoid unjustifiable dogmatism. What seems to be a fulfillment, or even a preparation for the fulfillment of Scripture may not be at all. Also, since the Bible clearly makes the return of Christ imminent we must not set up a scenario in which certain conditions must be met before Christ can return. Finally, date-setting must also be strenuously avoided. The Bible warns clearly against this.

> The threat of death for all who utter false predictions in the name of the Lord aside [Deut. 18:20–22], there are at least two points of application to today's doomsday prophets which we may draw from this text. First, such people presumptuously think they represent God. Second, such people are not sacrosanct; they need not terrify well-informed Christians with their alarmist warnings and empty promises. In any event, it is hard to place much confidence in today's prophetic seers who claim they know when Jesus will return when he himself does not; "No one knows about that day or hour, not even the angels in heaven, nor the Son, but only the Father" (Mark 13:32).[1]

Despite the scriptural warnings, some continue to make predictions and set dates as to when end-time events will unfold and Christ will return. Recently (April 1997), for example, Monte Judah, the editor of the newsletter of Lion and Lamb Ministries (not to be confused with the Lamb and Lion Ministries), said the signing of the peace security agreement in September 1993 at the White House indicated that we are in the middle of the Great Tribulation and the world would end soon. He predicted that the middle events of the seven-year period would all occur before March 23, 1997. None of them did! He later admitted he was wrong.

Numbers of Jewish scholars and rabbis as well as significant numbers of Gentiles have taught that the world will last six thousand years from the time of its creation. This view is based upon the six-day creation week in Genesis 1. At least four thousand years can be accounted for from Adam to Christ. We are about to enter the year 2000 which, of course, will make six thousand years of world history according to many. This certainly makes the year 2000 highly significant.

There will be a time when time will be no more. As we move closer to the next millennium it is only natural to ask what the year 2000 and the ones following that hold for our world.

Many who have no interest in spiritual things or Bible prophecy are predicting a bright, intriguing, and fascinating new millennium. Is that really an accurate prospect? Are we really on the edge of utopia? Is the world getting better and life made easier and more hopeful as we bask in all the technological and scientific discoveries and advances? Or are we going full speed toward the end of time? Does the year 2000 signal that the world is on the edge of a precipice? Are the end-time events so clearly predicted in the Bible about to unfold? According to U.S. intelligence sources, by the year 2000 at least twenty-four Third World nations such as Libya, Iraq, Syria, and Iran will have long-range ballistic missiles, many of these with nuclear capability.

With each passing year—even month, week, day, and moment—we are nearer the return of our Lord. The new millennium beginning in 2000 will introduce us to a new epoch of world history and the unfolding of God's sovereign plan for us and His world. Jesus may come by the year 2000, or during the new millennium. No one knows but God Himself. We do know we are to always be ready because He could come today. Are you ready? The way to be ready is to be in His family. The way to get in His family is to acknowledge yourself as a sinner and trust Christ alone to be your Substitute for sin. When you do that you will become a child of God and assured of heaven (John 1:12; 3:16).

One-World Church

Religionists began the drive to build a world church long ago. The history, theology, and goals of such organizations as the Federal Council of Christian Churches (1908), the National Council of Churches (1950), the World Council of Churches (1948), and the Consultation on Church Union (1960) bear abundant testimony to this fact.

The modern ecumenical movement has its roots in liberal theology with its denial of the essentials of the his-

toric orthodox Christian faith. Liberal theology, to take one
more step backward, was born in and grew out of the
man-centered philosophies of the Renaissance (1453–
1690) and periods which followed.

What is the goal of the contemporary liberal ecumenical movement among churches? Many in the movement have denied any desire to build a world church, a
one-world religion. Despite all the past and present protes-
tations, the goal seems clearly to be to create one church
for one world. Everything else must take second place to
the dream of ecumenists to bring all religions of the world
under one organizational structure, one religious umbrella.
This does seem to be preparing the way for what is described in Revelation 17.

The initial goal to build a world church remains in-
tact today. Sixty religious leaders from around the world
gathered in San Francisco recently, all seeking to sign a
charter of the United Religions. Episcopal Bishop William
Swing was quoted in the *San Francisco Chronicle* on June
20, 1996, as saying: "I am convinced that the time is ripe
for a global initiative to call the world's religions together.
. . . The whole world must get on board" to make this a reality, he said.

Konrad Raiser, the general secretary of the World
Council of Churches, has called for a council to settle doctrinal differences beginning in the year 2000. This universal council would have as its goal the resolving of the issues dividing the church (Ecumenical News International).

> In a further bid to bring the world to one point of view,
> there is now a movement afoot to establish a permanent
> "United Religions" (UR) organization. A charter setting

up the UN-style group is currently being drafted, and a facility to promote this point of view may well be open in the near future. Like the UN, the UR will have a five-hundred-member assembly, a thirty-six-member executive council, and a secretary general. Comprised of representatives of religions both large and small, the group would meet once or twice a year to "reverse the use of religion to justify war, hate, violence, aggression, and intolerance." Peacemaker teams of spiritual leaders and conflict-resolution specialists would be dispatched to trouble spots throughout the world. The origins of UR—perhaps the predecessor to the global church prophesied in the Bible—are in the World Parliament of Religions, which has already convened to adopt "a new world ethic."[2]

Some who for years have trafficked in evangelical circles share similar views with liberals: "God has been at work saving human beings before Jesus was born and does so where Jesus is not named. . . . I welcome the Siva Siddhartha literature of Hinduism, which celebrates a personal God of love, and the emphasis on grace that I see in Japanese Shin-Sha sect. I also support the Buddha as a figure in the style of the Old Testament" (Clark Pinnock, *More Than One Way*).

One World Government

Paralleling the goal of building a world church and closely associated with it has been the dream of a world government as well. This has always been true. Thirty years ago a staff member of the Foundation for Economic Education put it this way: "Influential churchmen and theologians operating through official church agencies and organizations have strained to the task of molding the Protestant churches into a politically potent Great Church for the Great Society. Their joint efforts have not been for the attainment of Christian unity for its own sake; it has been unity—for the sake—of power."[3]

The idea of a one-world government is heralded as the only way to "save" the world. Our planet, we are told, has no hope without global participation. A Nobel Prize-winning economist, Jan Tinbregen, put it this way: "Mankind's problems can no longer be solved by national governments. What is needed is a world government. This can best be achieved by strengthening the United Nations system."

There are other harbingers of a future one-world government. Former Soviet dictator Mikhail Gorbachev's blueprint for such a government and his book, *The Search for a New Beginning: Developing a New Civilization,* discussed at the five-day meeting in San Francisco with world and political leaders several years ago, is certainly one such harbinger. Other organizations and movements such as the World Constitution and Parliament Association in Colorado, Warstop, Philadelphia II, and New Age religious groups are but a few with the same agenda.

Talk of a biochip implant for all the world's citizens is becoming more and more popular. Due to the unauthorized border crossings from Mexico into California, that state has been looking with increased interest at the probability of a biochip. Governor Pete Wilson and Senator Dianne Feinstein have both agreed the time has come for a national identity card called MARC standing for, "Multi-technology Automated Reader Card."

Feinstein has called on her colleagues in the U.S. Congress to make carrying such a card mandatory for every American citizen. Her remarks, memorialized in the *Daily Washington Journal Roll Call,* are chilling in their content: "I believe that a new, phone- or machine-readable card that all job benefits applicants would be required to present to verify their work or eligibility for assistance deserves careful consideration. As (the Senate Subcommittee on Immigration) heard (from representatives of the State Department, INS, FBI, Social Security Administration, Secret Service, state and motor vehicle authorities), counterfeit-resistant cards that incorporate 'biometric' data are available and in use today. Whether the card carries a magnetic strip on which the bearer's unique voice, retina pattern, or fingerprint is digitally encoded, or whether it incorporates a digitized photo and signature integrated into the plastic card itself, it is clear to me that state-of-the-art work and benefits eligibility IDs can and must replace the Dinosaur Age documents now being used."[4]

Rabin Forney, staff writer for the *Daily News* in Lebanon, Pennsylvania, November 18, 1996, set forth his dream of a world government: "Our vision of the future should be one of a single, united globe, controlled by a centralized government, possessing a single currency, and possessing the wisdom and tolerance to allow for basic freedoms for all people on the Earth." He went on to say, "Having a global government does not mean an end to national feelings. There can still be a United States of America, there can still be a Canada, a Russia, a China, a Gabon. But there can be a single authority in existence of which all nations are a part." The title of Forney's piece says it all: "Global Unison Only Way to World Peace." This in an editorial in a small-town newspaper.

All such efforts toward a one-world government seem clearly to be preparations for what is described in Revelation 18.

How Should We Then Live?

So maybe there will not be a one-world church or one-world government before Jesus returns. We cannot be sure of that. We can be sure, though, that Jesus is coming again. The human writers of the New Testament and the early Christians believed He could come in their lifetime. We should believe that too. If we really do believe it, our living will be affected.

I have on my desk a small motto which faces the entrance door. It reads "Perhaps Today." This is a reminder that Jesus could come to take His own to be with Him at any time. Because this is true, each of us who claims Jesus as our Substitute for sin should be ready to appear before Him any moment. We need to keep short accounts with God. Unconfessed sin should not weigh us down. Broken fellowship with God and others needs to be restored. The hope we Christians have ought to be shared with others by our lives and by our lips. Indeed, God wants us to be light and salt in this dark and corrupt world.

Imagine you just got word that someone very important to you is coming to your house. Your friends are not sure of the exact time of their arrival, but they assured you it could be any time on the last Saturday of the month. This news comes to you and your family as a complete shock. It has been fifteen years since you and your wife last saw these folks. Your two youngest children have never even seen them or their children. As the time draws near, what would you do to be ready for the visit? Special cleaning—inside and out—would certainly be done. Plenty of food would have to be brought in—special delicacies and only the best of everything would be gathered. These are special people. You have been honored to be on their list of friends whom they want to visit. Above everything else, you want to be completely ready when they arrive.

God has sent us a letter in the Bible. He has promised that His Son would come again just as surely as He came the first time, hundreds of years after His coming had been predicted. He expects us to be ready for His coming. He has not told us exactly when He will come, but He did promise that He would come again. We are to live in an expectancy mode, anticipating, looking for Him at all times to return. It could be today! This day may in fact be the last day before Jesus comes again.

Appendix

Complementary Hermeneutics

Recently, some who claim to be interpreting Scripture literally have introduced what they call "complementary hermeneutics." Those who use this approach classify themselves as progressive dispensationalists.[1] They also still wish to be numbered among premillennial pretribulation dispensationalists (see pp. 57–62). Darrell Bock, who seems to have been the one who introduced the term "progressive dispensationalism," defines it this way: "The New Testament does introduce change and advance; it does not merely repeat Old Testament revelation. In making complementary additions, however, it does not jettison old promises."[2]

The method at the present time does not seem to be applied to all of Scripture, but is applied to the promise of the Davidic covenant of 2 Samuel 7. It is admitted that when the covenant was originally given, it was made exclusively with Israel. However, in Acts 2 on the Day of Pentecost, Peter brought in the church as recipients of the covenant as well. This is defended by Peter's use of Psalm 110. In this way it is "inferred" or "implied" that the kingdom promises to Israel are now being fulfilled in part by Christ's position at the right hand of the Father. This means the Davidic kingdom is "now but not yet" in all its fullness. What the New Testament is said to have done is "complement" here what was given in the Old Testament.

What this means, if applied unilaterally to all of Scripture, is that the original recipients of the revelation could never know precisely what the text meant until the promise was fulfilled or the canon of Scripture was closed. After all, later "complements" might introduce drastic changes in the original promise.

"Complementary hermeneutics" must not be confused with the historic orthodox doctrine of progressive revelation. This latter truth means that God revealed His truth gradually, sometimes over a long period of time. What was revealed later never changed the original revelation, however. The meaning and the recipients of the promise always remain the same. More truth is simply given about the germ truth given initially. When a promise was given to certain people about a certain thing or certain place, it was always fulfilled exactly as predicted.

Robert L. Thomas has given an excellent critique of progressive dispensationalism and especially its complementary hermeneutics. It appears in an important book dealing with the last days of the church on earth.[3]

All the biblical and theological ramifications of progressive dispensationalism and its foundation stone of complementary hermeneutics have not yet surfaced. Several have, but the effects even of these upon classic or normal dispensationalism have not yet been realized. Two doctrines which are absolutely indispensable to the system out of which progressive dispensationalism arose and with which its advocates still want to be identified are greatly affected by it. These are the mystery nature of the church and the baptizing work of the Holy Spirit. Progressive dispensationalism slights both of these by attaching new meanings to them.

Progressive dispensationalists no longer believe that the church is a mystery completely unrevealed in the Old Testament. "Mystery," as used in the New Testament, has always been understood to mean that which had not been made known before but came to be made known. This meaning is based on Paul's usage of the word in Romans 16:25. Progressive dispensationalism does not believe the church was completely unrevealed in the Old Testament but that it was simply unrecognized there.

Likewise, progressives do not believe the baptizing work of the Holy Spirit is entirely new to the New Testament. They see shadows of the work of the Spirit in the Old Testament.

Many who are classic dispensationalists—and even those who are not dispensationalists at all—question why those who no longer believe in the foundational essentials of dispensationalism still want to be a part of the dispensationalism family.

This is truly something not yet revealed.

Notes

Part 1—The Issues

Chapter 1—Another Book on Prophecy?

1. *The Fundamentals—A Testimony to the Truth* (Chicago: Testimony Publishing Company, 1909).
2. See the author's *Neo-Evangelicalism Today* (Shaumburg, IL: Regular Baptist Press, 1978) for a description of a rather new variation called NeoEvangelicalism within which there are those who deny the total inerrancy of Scripture.
3. John F. Walvoord, *The Millennial Kingdom* (Findlay, OH: Dunham Publishing Company, 1959), 3.
4. John Bright, *The Kingdom of God* (Nashville: Abingdon, 1953), 1, 7, 197.

Chapter 2—Evangelical Agreement on Things to Come

1. Lewis Sperry Chafer, *Systematic Theology* (Dallas: Dallas Seminary Press, 1947), IV, 256.
2. A new work by a well-known and greatly respected premillennial writer dealing with all the significant prophecies of Scripture in the order in which they appear in the Bible is *Prophecy Knowledge Handbook* by John F. Walvoord (Wheaton, IL: Victor Books, 1990).
3. Charles C. Ryrie, *The Bible and Tomorrow's News* (Wheaton, IL: Scripture Press Publications, Incorporated, 1969), 58–59.
4. Loraine Boettner, *Immortality* (Philadelphia: Presbyterian and Reformed Publishing Co., 1962), 59.
5. Ibid., 91.
6. Rudolf Bultmann, *Kerygma and Myth* (London: SPCK, 1954), 4.

7. Lesley H. Woodson, *Hell and Salvation* (Old Tappan, NJ: Fleming H. Revell Company, 1973), 24.
8. Ron Devillier, *Real,* Spring 1972.

Part 2—Systems of Eschatology: How Evangelicals Differ

Chapter 3—Premillennialism

1. C. H. Dodd, *The Parables of the Kingdom* (New York: Charles Scribner Sons, 1961), 50.
2. Charles C. Ryrie, *The Basis of the Premillennial Faith* (New York: Loizeaux Brothers, 1953), 12.
3. John F. Walvoord, *The Rapture Question* (Findlay, OH: Dunham Publishing Co., 1957), 49.
4. Charles C. Ryrie, *Dispensationalism Today* (Chicago: Moody Press, 1965), 29.
5. Ibid., 31.
6. Diagrams 2–4, 6, and 8–11 also appear in my *Evangelical Theology* (Grand Rapids: Kregel Publications, 1986).
7. Alexander Reese, *The Approaching Advent of Christ* (London: Marshall, Morgan & Scott, Ltd., 1975), 18.
8. George L. Rose, *Tribulation Till Translation* (Glendale, CA: Rose Publishing Co., 1943), 68–69.
9. George H. Fromow, *Will the Church Pass Through the Great Tribulation?* (London: The Sovereign Grace Advent Testimony, n.d.), 1.
10. George E. Ladd, *Blessed Hope* (Grand Rapids: Eerdmans, 1956), 72–77; and Robert H. Gundry, *The Church and the Tribulation* (Grand Rapids: Zondervan, 1973).
11. A recent exception to this is R. H. Gundry in his *The Church and the Tribulation,* 12–28.
12. Norman B. Harrison, *The End* (Minneapolis: The Harrison Service, 1941), 118.
13. Gleason L. Archer, "Jesus Is Coming Again: Midtribulation," *Christian Life* (May 1974), 21.

14. Ray Brubaker, "The Purpose of the Tribulation," *Radar News* (December, 1968), 6.

Chapter 4—Amillennialism

1. J. G. Voss, *Blue Banner Faith and Life* (January–March, 1951), cited from Loraine Boettner, *The Millennium* (The Presbyterian and Reformed Publishing Co., 1964), 109.
2. Jay Adams, *The Time Is at Hand* (Nutley, NJ: The Presbyterian and Reformed Publishing Co., 1966), 8.
3. Ibid., 9.
4. For a presentation and defense of covenant theology from the perspective of an advocate, see L. Berkhof, *Systematic Theology,* (Grand Rapids: Wm. B. Eerdmans, 1968), 262–304. For a critique of covenant theology from the perspective of a dispensational opponent, see Charles Ryrie, *Dispensationalism Today* (Chicago: Moody, Press, 1965), 177–191.
5. George N. M. Collins, "Covenant Theology," *Baker's Dictionary of Theology* (Grand Rapids: Baker Book House, 1960), 144.

Chapter 5—Postmillennialism

1. Augustus Hopkins Strong, *Systematic Theology* (Philadelphia: American Baptist Publication Society, 1907), III, 1010–1011.
2. Loraine Boettner, *The Millennium* (Philadelphia: Presbyterian and Reformed Publishing Co., 1964), 4, 14.
3. Principal sources of information for this are: The Chalcedon Foundation and *The Journal of Christian Reconstruction.* Some significant publications promoting it are Greg. L. Bahnsen, *Theonomy in Christian Ethics;* Rousas J. Rushdoony, *The Institutes of Biblical Law* (Phillipsburg, NJ: Presbyterian and Reformed Publishing Co., 1988), and *God's Plan for Victory* (Fairfax, VA: Thoburn Press, 1977).
4. See this author's articles in *Bibliotheca Sacra* (January–March 1986, April–June 1986 and July–September 1986) on

"Theonomy and Dispensationalism." Also see Thomas D. Ice, "An Evaluation of Theonomic Neopostmillennialism" in *Bibliotheca Sacra* (July–September 1988). An outstanding exception is John Jefferson Davis's work—*Christ's Victorious Kingdom—Postmillennialism Reconsidered,* Baker Book House, 1986. Davis is postmillennial but does not embrace the theonomy-reconstructionist viewpoint.

5. R. Laird Harris, "Theonomy in Christian Ethics" *Covenant Seminary Review* 5 (1979), 1.
6. Greg Bahnsen, *Theonomy in Christian Ethics* (Phillipsburg, NJ: Presbyterian and Reformed Publishing Co., 1977), 82.
7. Ibid., 427, 439, 445, 466 ff.

Chapter 6—What Are the Differences?

1. Arthur D. Katterjohn, *The Rapture—When?* (Wheaton, IL: Arthur D. Katterjohn, 1975) 60.
2. Louis DeCaro, *Israel Today: Fulfillment of Prophecy* (Philadelphia: Presbyterian and Reformed Publishing Co., 1974). This entire volume presents this thesis.
3. See for example Oswald T. Allis, *Prophecy and the Church* (Philadelphia: Presbyterian and Reformed Publishing Co., 1945); William E. Cox, *An Examination of Dispensationalism* (Philadelphia: Presbyterian and Reformed Publishing Company, 1963); Clarence B. Bass, *Backgrounds to Dispensationalism* (Grand Rapids: Eerdman's Publishing Company, 1950). See Norman Kraus, *Dispensationalism in America* (Richmond, VA: John Knox Press, 1958), and the writings of Dave McPherson (Kansas City, MO: Heart of America Bible Society).
4. Oswald T. Allis, "Modern Dispensationalism and the Doctrine of the Unity of the Scriptures," *The Evangelical Quarterly* 8 (January 1936), 24.
5. Oswald T. Allis, *Prophecy and the Church,* 48.
6. Op. cit., 3.
7. Ibid.

8. C. F. Hogg and W. E. Vine, *Church and the Tribulation* (London: Pickering and Inglis Ltd., 1938), 11.

9. Charles C. Ryrie, *Dispensationalism Today* (Chicago: Moody Press, 1965), 110–31.

10. C. Daniel Payton Fuller, "The Hermeneutics of Dispensationalism" (Unpublished doctoral dissertation, Northern Baptist Theological Seminary in Chicago, 1957) and also Cox, *Amillennialism Today* (Phillipsburg, NJ: Presbyterian and Reformed Publishing Co., 1966), for examples.

11. J. E. Adams, *The Time is at Hand* (Philadelphia: Presbyterian and Reformed Publishing Co., 1974), 7.

12. Ibid., 7.

13. Cox, *Amillennialism Today* (Philadelphia: Presbyterian and Reformed Publishing Co., 1956), 15. Quoted from John F. Walvoord, *The Millennial Kingdom* (Findley, OH: Dunham Publishing Company, 1959), 59.

14. Op. cit., Cox, 15–16.

15. Alva J. McClain, *The Greatness of the Kingdom* (Chicago: Moody Press, 1968), 139–46; Paul Lee Tan, *The Interpretation of Prophecy* (Winona Lake, IN: B. M. H. Books, 1974), 275–77, and Walvoord, *The Millennial Kingdom,* 3–17.

16. See an example of this in Hal Lindsey, *The Late Great Planet Earth* (Grand Rapids: Zondervan, 1970). In great outline, this book presents the pretribulational position but not all who embrace the view share Lindsey's dogmatism in certain areas.

Part 3—Why the Variant Views of Things to Come?

Chapter 7—Interpreting Scripture

1. Bernard Ramm, *Protestant Biblical Interpretation* (Boston: W. A. Wilde Co., 1950), 1.

2. For a discussion of more recent differences some evangelicals want to make between inspiration and inerrancy, see Harold Lindsell's *The Battle for the Bible* (Grand Rapids:

The Zondervan Corporation, 1976), and his *The Bible in the Balance* (Grand Rapids: The Zondervan Corporation, 1979). Also see *Inerrancy,* edited by Norman L. Geisler, Zondervan, 1979).

3. I recommend the following for study in this area. Zuck, Roy B. *Basic Bible Interpretation.* Wheaton, IL: Victor Books, 1991 and Johnson, Elliott. *Expository Hermeneutics: An Introduction.* Grand Rapids: Zondervan, 1990.

4. Oswald T. Allis, *Prophecy and the Church* (Philadelphia: Presbyterian and Reformed Pub. Co., 1945), 238.

5. William E. Cox, *Amillennialism Today* (Philadelphia: Presbyterian & Reformed Pub. Co., 1966), 13.

6. Jay Adams, *The Time Is at Hand* (Nutley, NJ: Presbyterian and Reformed Pub. Co., 1966), 13.

7. Loraine Boettner, *The Millennium* (Philadelphia: Presbyterian and Reformed Pub. Co., 1964), 82.

8. George N. H. Peters, *The Theocratic Kingdom of Our Lord Jesus the Christ* (Grand Rapids: Kregel Publications, 1957), 47.

9. John F Walvoord, *The Millennial Kingdom* (Findlay, OH: Dunham Publishing Co., 1959), 59.

10. See Milton S. Terry, *Biblical Hermeneutics* (Grand Rapids: Zondervan Publishing House, 1969), 163–74 for other methods.

11. Bernard Ramm, *Protestant Biblical Interpretation* (Boston: W. A. Wilde, Co., 1950), 53.

12. Ibid., 64.

13. Examples of these may be found in J. Dwight Pentecost, *Things to Come* (Findlay, OH: Dunham Publishing Co., 1958), 9–15, and Paul Lee Tan, *The Interpretation of Prophecy* (Winona Lake, IN: B. M. H. Books, Inc., 1974), 29–39.

14. Charles C. Ryrie, *Dispensationalism Today* (Chicago: Moody Press, 1965), 87– 88.

15. Allis, op. cit., 17.

16. Ibid., 17–18.

17. Pentecost, op. cit., 14–15.

18. Ramm, op. cit., 23.
19. Ibid., 21.
20. See Meno J. Brunk, *Fulfilled Prophecies* (Krockette, KY: Rod & Staff Publications, Inc., 1971).

Chapter 8—The Methods of Interpretation and the Covenants

1. Within dispensational premillennialism there are those who appear to have accepted the nondispensational premillennial view of the Davidic kingdom. In fact some of the same or very similar terminology appears in their writings. They write about the kingdom that is "already and not yet" and about the "invisible" and "visible" kingdom of God. Though they do not want to be identified with the covenant premillennialism of George Eldon Ladd, their view is strikingly similar and almost indistinguishable from it.

   Here are some examples in which the relation of the Davidic and New Covenants to the present church age is being discussed. "The New Covenant itself stands inaugurated, but not totally consummated. It is only initially consummated. The rule of Jesus from God's right hand initially yet decisively fulfills promises made to David" (Darrell Bock, "The Reign of the Lord Christ," Unpublished paper, Post ETS copy, Dec. 1987, 19). Another dispensational premillennialist writes, "Though the emphasis of the teaching of Jesus was on the futurity of the kingdom, His total message concerning the kingdom also included its presence and the possibility of men and women entering the kingdom now" (Robert L. Saucy, *Bibliotheca Sacra,* "The Presence of the Kingdom and the Life of the Church," [January–March, 1988, 36]). For the covenant premillennial view of the same issue see George Eldon Ladd in Clouse, Robert G. in *The Meaning of the Millennium, InterVarsity Press, 1977.*

Two recent books which set forth progressive dispensationalism are Craig Blaising and Darrell Bock, *Dispensationalism, Israel and the Church* (Grand Rapids: Zondervan, 1992), and Craig Blaising and Darrell Bock, *Progressive Dispensationalism* (Wheaton, IL: Victor Books, 1993). A book which critiques progressive dispensationalism is Wesley Willis and John Master, editors, *Issues in Dispensationalism* (Chicago: Moody Press, 1994).

2. John F. Walvoord, *The Millennial Kingdom* (Findlay, OH: Dunham Publishing Co., 1959), 151.

3. Ibid., 150–52.

4. Lewis Sperry Chafer, *Systematic Theology* (Dallas: Dallas Seminary Press, 1948),IV, 317.

5. Pentecost, op. cit., 104.

6. Ryrie, *The Basis of the Premillennial Faith* (New York: Loizeaux Bros., 1953), 112.

7. Though not transferred to the church, Israel's promises of the coming kingdom are shared by the church at the present time according to progressive dispensationalism.

8. Ryrie, op. cit.

9. Ibid., 125.

10. Allis, op. cit., 32–36.

11. William Cox, *Biblical Studies in Final Things* (Philadelphia: Presbyterian and Reformed Publishing Co., 1967), 7.

12. Ibid., 8.

13. Louis A. DeCaro, *Israel Today: Fulfillment of Prophecy?* (Philadelphia: Presbyterian and Reformed Publishing Co., 1974), 64, 65.

14. Boettner, op. cit., 123.

15. Ibid., 102–3.

16. J. Marcellus Kik, *Revelation Twenty—An Exposition* (Philadelphia: Presbyterian and Reformed Publishing Co., 1955), 29.

17. Ibid., 45–46.

18. Charles Hodge, *Systematic Theology* (Grand Rapids: Wm. B. Eerdmans Publishing Co., 1968), III, 810.

19. David Chilton, *The Days of Vengeance An Exposition of the Book of Revelation* (Ft. Worth, TX: Dominion Press, 1987), 587.

Chapter 9—Why the Differences Persist

1. Arthur D. Katterjohn, *The Rapture—When?* (Wheaton, IL: Arthur D. Katterjohn, 220 East Union, 1975), 1.

2. Robert H. Gundry in his book *The Church and the Tribulation* (Grand Rapids: Zondervan, 1973) illustrates this a number of times by showing how certain passages may be used to support both pre- and posttribulationism and are not determinative in themselves.

Part 4—What Can I Do?

Chapter 10—Steps Toward a Solution

1. C. Stanley Lowell, *The Ecumenical Mirage* (Grand Rapids: Baker Book House, 1967), 65–67.

Chapter 11—Be Ready: The New Millennium and the Second Coming of Christ

1. Pate, C. Marvin and Calvin B. Haines Jr. *Doomsday Delusions* (Downers Grove, IL: InterVarsity Press, 1995).

2. Van Impe, Jack. *2001: On the Edge of Eternity* (Dallas: Word Publishing, 1996).

3. Ingersalson, Kenneth W., compiler. *Your Church—Their Target* (Arlington, VA: Better Books Publisher, 1966).

4. Ibid.

Appendix

1. This movement has been discussed briefly in this volume, pages 132–35.

2. Craig Blaising and Darrell L. Bock, "Dispensationalism, Israel and the Church: Assessment and Dialogue," *Dispensa-*

      tionalism, Israel and the Church (Grand Rapids: Zondervan, 1992), 392–93.

3. Robert L. Thomas, "A Critique of Dispensational Hermeneutics," Thomas Ice and Timothy Demy, editors. *When the Trumpet Sounds* (Eugene, OR: Harvest House Publishers, 1995), 413–25.

Annotated Bibliography

The following annotated bibliography has been divided into three categories—Beginner's Level, Intermediate Level, and the Advanced Level. In this way the reader will be able to find those books which will meet his particular need.

Amillennialism

Beginner's Level
Adams, Jay. *The Time is at Hand.* Philadelphia: Presbyterian and Reformed Publishing Co., 1974. 123 pp. Presentation of positive statement of the amillennial position as an orderly system.

Intermediate Level
Cox, William E. *Amillennialism Today.* Philadelphia: Presbyterian and Reformed Publishing Co., 1966. 143 pp. Presents the amillennial view of crucial doctrines related to eschatology.

Advanced Level
Allis, O. T. *Prophecy and the Church.* Philadelphia: Presbyterian and Reformed Publishing Co., 1945. 339 pp. An examination and rejection of the dispensationist claim that the church is a mystery. A claim that the Old Testament promises to Israel are fulfilled by the church.

Hamilton, Floyd E. *The Basis of Millennial Faith.* Grand Rapids: William B. Eerdmans Publishing Company, 1942. 160 pp. An attempt to present amillennialism as a system of belief and to show it is orthodox.

Postmillennialism

Beginner's Level
Boettner, Loraine. *The Millennium.* Philadelphia: Presbyterian and Reformed Publishing Co., 1964. 380 pp. Postmillennialism, amillennialism, and premillennialism are presented. Author argues in favor of postmillennialism.

Intermediate Level
DeMar, Gary. *The Debate Over Christian Reconstruction.* Dominion Press, 1988. The author sets forth a defense of Christian reconstructionism and postmillennialism.

House, H. Wayne and Ice, Thomas. *Dominion Theology: Blessing or Curse?* Multnomah, 1988. This is a critique of Theonomy and contemporary postmillennialism from two dispensational premillennialists.

Kik, Jay M. *Matthew 24* and *Revelation 20.* Philadelphia: Presbyterian and Reformed Publishing Co., 1948, 1955 respectively. 97 pp. and 92 pp. respectively. In these two books the author argues for postmillennialism from these two crucial passages.

Advanced Level
Davis, John Jefferson. *Christ's Victorious Kingdom—Postmillennialism Reconsidered.* Baker, 1986. A scholarly defense of the system without embracing theonomy and reconstructionism.

Premillennialism

Beginner's Level
Feinberg, Charles L. *Premillennialism or Amillennialism.* Wheaton, IL: Van Kampen Press, 1954. 354 pp. The systems are compared and contrasted with each other. Author argues for premillennialism.

Ryrie, Charles C. *The Basis of Premillennial Faith.* New York: Loizeaux Brothers, 1953. 160 pp. Well-outlined defense of premillennialism.

Intermediate Level

Pentecost, J. Dwight. *Things to Come.* Grand Rapids: Zondervan Publishing Company, 1958. 633 pp. Most complete presentation of premillennial, pretribulational eschatology. Presents opposing views with author's refutations.

Walvoord, John F. *The Millennial Kingdom.* Findlay, OH: Dunham Publishing Company, 1959. 373 pp. Comprehensive treatment of the millennial systems. Author builds case for premillennialism from Scripture and history.

Advanced Level

Clouse, Robert G., Ed. *The Meaning of the Millennium.* InterVarsity Press, 1977. 223 pp. Historic premillennialism, dispensational premillennialism, postmillennialism, and amillennialism are presented by advocates of these positions. Opponents then respond to each of the positions.

McClain, Alva J. *The Greatness of the Kingdom.* Chicago: Moody Press, 1968. 566 pp. Traces idea of mediatorial kingdom through the Bible. Places strong emphasis upon premillennialism. A classic.

Pentecost, J. Dwight. *Thy Kingdom Come.* Wheaton, IL: Victor Books, 1990, 360 pp. Traces God's rule from eternity past to eternity future. The author demonstrates that God's kingdom program is the outworking of His unconditional covenants.

Peters, George N. H., *The Theocratic Kingdom,* 3 vols., Kregel, 2180 pp.

Midtribulationism

Beginner's Level

Archer, Gleason L. "Jesus Is Coming Again." *Christian Life,* May 1974, p. 21f.

Rosenthal, Marvin. *The Prewrath Rapture of the Church.* Nashville: Thomas Nelson, 1990. The view presented is more closely associated with the midtribulational view than with any of the other options. The author's major contention is that the seal judgments do not represent God's wrath, and the Rapture and Second Coming are not separate events.

226   The Last Days Handbook

Intermediate Level
Harrison, Norman B. *The End.* Minneapolis: Harrison Service, 1941. 239 pp. Defense for the Rapture in the middle of Daniel's seventieth week.

Partial Rapturism

Beginner's Level
Brubaker, Ray. *The Purpose of the Great Tribulation.* St. Petersburg, FL, 1968. 8 pp. Also other pamphlets. Viewing one of the purposes of the Tribulation as a means of testing lukewarm Christians, the author argues his case for partial rapturism.

Advanced Level
Lang, G. H. *The Revelation of Jesus Christ.* London: Oliphants, 1945. 420 pp. Most complete and comprehensive presentation of the partial Rapture position available.

Posttribulationism

Beginner's Level
Ladd, George E. *The Blessed Hope.* Grand Rapids: Zondervan Publishing Company, 1956. 167 pp. Defines the blessed hope not as deliverance from the Tribulation but preservation through it. A premillennial posttribulational defense.

Intermediate Level
Reese, Alexander. *The Approaching Advent of Christ.* London: Marshall, Morgan & Scott, n.d. 328 pp. A classic posttribulational polemic.

Advanced Level
Gundry, Robert H. *The Church and the Tribulation.* Grand Rapids: Zondervan Publishing Company, 1973. 224 pp. Most recent and exegetically based defense of premillennial posttribulationism. Author seeks to build his case by showing that passages often used in defense of pretribulationism may also be used to support posttribulationism.

Payne, Jay Barton. *The Imminent Appearing of Christ.* Grand Rapids: William B. Eerdmans Publishing Company, 1962. 191

pp. Presents a new view of imminency that the author feels is in harmony with posttribulationism.

Pretribulationism

Beginner's Level

English, E. Schuyler. *Rethinking the Rapture.* Travelers Rest, SC: Southern Bible Book House, 1954. 123 pp. Brief and concise defense of pretribulationism.

Walvoord, John F. *The Rapture Question.* Grand Rapids: Zondervan Publishing Company, 1957. 204 pp. The various views respecting the time of the Rapture and the participants in it are presented. Author sets forth arguments used in defense of the position and concludes by giving fifty arguments for pretribulationism.

Intermediate Level

Wood, Leon J. *Is the Rapture Next?* Grand Rapids: Zondervan Publishing Company, 1956. 120 pp. A solid defense of pretribulationism. Deals with crucial issues.

Advanced Level

Showers, Renald E. *Maranatha.* Bellmawr, NJ: Friends of Israel Gospel Ministry, Inc., 1995. This work is scholarly and is a thorough defense of the pretribulational view. Stress is upon the doctrine of imminency. It is the most extensive and definitive work to date setting forth the imminent hope of Christ's return for His own and refuting the pre-wrath view of Marvin Rosenthal.

Ice, Thomas and Demy, Timothy, editors. *When the Trumpet Sounds.* Eugene, OR: Harvest House Publishers, 1995. A wide gamut of issues is discussed, with an emphasis on alerting the reader to the urgency of the hour and the need for preparation in view of the imminent hope.

Antidispensationalism

Beginner's Level

Cox, William E. *An Examination of Dispensationalism.* Philadelphia: Presbyterian and Reformed Publishing Company, 1963.

61 pp. Author finds problems with dispensational beliefs and with early spokesmen of the view.

Intermediate Level

Bass, Clarence B. *Backgrounds to Dispensationalism.* Grand Rapids: William B. Eerdmans Publishing Company, 1960. 184 pp. An attempted refutation of the dispensational system by appealing to its recency and by showing flaws in one of the earliest spokesmen for the system.

Kraus, C. Norman. *Dispensationalism in America.* Richmond, VA: John Knox Press, 1958. 156 pp. Deals with the rise of dispensationalism and the relation of dispensationalism to premillennialism.

Advanced Level

Bahnsen, Greg L. and Gentry, Kenneth L. Jr., *House Divided: The Break-Up of Dispensational Theology.* Tyler, TX: Institute for Christian Economics, 1989. 411 pp. Authors seek to expose and explore differences among dispensationalists in an attempt to discredit the system.

Dispensationalism

Beginner's Level

Barndollar, Walker W. *The Validity of Dispensationalism.* Des Plaines, IL: Regular Baptist Press, 1964. 47 pp. Shows the logic and biblical base for dispensationalism.

Chafer, Lewis Sperry. *Dispensations.* Dallas: Dallas Theological Seminary Press, 1936. 108 pp. In this volume the founder of Dallas Theological Seminary presents a brief statement of the relation of dispensationalism to other vital doctrines.

Intermediate Level

Ryrie, Charles C. *Dispensationalism.* Chicago: Moody Press, 1995.

Chafer, Lewis Sperry. *Systematic Theology,* 4 volumes. Grand Rapids: Kregel Publications, 1993.

Willis, Wesley and Master, John, editors. *Issues in Dispensationalism.* Chicago: Moody Press, 1994. Some of the ramifications of progressive dispensationalism as it affects other doctrines are described and highlighted in this volume.

Advanced Level

Poythress, Vern S. *Understanding Dispensationalists.* Grand Rapids: Zondervan, 1987. This is a friendly evaluation and critique of dispensationalism by one who does not embrace the system.

Showers, Renald E. *There Really Is a Difference! A Comparison of Covenant and Dispensational Theology.* Bellmawr, NJ: Friends of Israel Gospel Ministry, Inc., 1990. Both systems are examined and evaluated. The author builds a case for dispensational theology.

Biblical Interpretation

Beginner's Level

Tan, Paul Lee. *The Interpretation of Prophecy.* Winona Lake, IN: BMH Books Incorporated, 1974. 435 pp. A detailed defense for the literal interpretation of prophecy.

Intermediate Level

Ramm, Bernard. *Protestant Biblical Interpretation.* Boston: W. A. Wilde Company, 1950. 197 pp. A standard text on the interpretation of Scripture in general.

Advanced Level

Johnson, Elliott. *Expository Hermeneutics: An Introduction.* Zondervan, 1990. The author described this excellent work in these words:

"Hermeneutics is a discipline whose importance is recognized in the process of Bible study. All believers have the opportunity and responsibility to read and interpret their Bibles and hermeneutics helps to bring normative control to that study of the text. This normative control rests in a literal system of interpretation which includes principles of grammatical, historical, literary, and theological contexts of interpretation."

Zuck, Roy B. *Basic Bible Interpretation.* Wheaton, IL: Victor Books, 1991. This is a scholarly yet reader-friendly study of how to interpret the Bible. The work is true to its title. All the bases are covered in clear understandable language. It is a gold mine of information and helps on how to understand the Bible. The literal or normal method of interpretation is championed.

Glossary

Abrahamic Covenant—The covenant or compact God made with Abraham promising him unconditionally a land, seed, and blessing.

Amillennialism—The system of theology which does not include a future millennial reign of Christ on the earth.

Biblical Covenants—The major ones are the Abrahamic, Davidic, Palestinian, and New. These are in contrast to the Theological Covenants described below.

Biblical Universalism—A belief that comes between eternal torment for the unregenerate and universalism. The view holds that God assigns irrevocable death to the unregenerate but not eternal punishment.

Bodily Resurrection—When used of Christ this means He arose in the same body, though glorified, which was crucified and buried.

Chiliasm—Belief in millennialism.

Conservative—Describes one who holds to the historic Christian faith.

Davidic Covenant—Covenant which enlarges the seed portion of the Abrahamic covenant.

Davidic Kingdom—The earthly messianic kingdom promised to David to be fulfilled by Christ.

Dispensationalism—A system of theology which takes into account the different programs of God and the different ways He has dealt with man.

Eschatology—The study of last things, end-times events.

Eternal State—The condition which will prevail after the thousand-year kingdom.

Evangelical—Describes one who embraces the historic orthodox Christian faith.

Fundamentalism—The viewpoint which not only holds to the historic Christian faith but also believes it should be defended and fought for.

Great Tribulation—Refers to the future seven-year period of unprecedented trouble, also called Daniel's seventieth week. Some apply this term to the last half of the "week."

Great White Throne Judgment—The judgment at which all the unregenerate of all time will appear.

Hermeneutics—The science of biblical interpretation.

Imminency—The belief that Christ could return at any moment.

Immortality—Belief in the eternal existence of the soul.

Intermediate State—The state between death and the Resurrection.

Judgment Seat of Christ—The judgment at which believers of this age will appear.

Kingdom—Used variously in Scripture to refer to reign. Context determines the reign.

Liberals—Describes those in theological circles who do not embrace the historic orthodox Christian faith.

Midtribulationism—Belief that Christ will return for the church in the Rapture in the middle of the future Tribulation.

Modernists—Term used to describe liberals in theology at the turn of the century.

New Covenant—The covenant which enlarges the blessing portion of the Abrahamic covenant.

Normative or Classic Dispensationalism—This term is used to describe historic dispensationalism which has always distinguished between God's program with Israel and His program with the church. It is the view which believes the church is a complete mystery in the Old Testament and was formed by the baptizing work of the Holy Spirit on the Day of Pentecost. Christ is not now on the throne of David but He is on the right hand of the Father's throne.

Palestinian Covenant—The covenant which enlarges the land portion of the Abrahamic covenant.

Partial Rapturism—Belief that only the spiritual Christians will be raptured when Christ returns.

Postmillennialism—Belief that Christ will return after the Church has Christianized society.

Posttribulationism—Belief that Christ will return for the church after the seventieth week of Daniel.

Premillennialism—That system of theology which believes Christ will return with His saints to establish the earthly kingdom promised to David.

Pretribulationism—Belief that Christ will return and rapture the entire church before any part of the seventieth week of Daniel begins.

Progressive Dispensationalism—The term used by those who still wish to be called dispensationalists but who do not believe some of the most basic essentials of dispensationalism. They do not believe God has a program for Israel and one for the church. They believe Christ is presently on the throne of David in heaven and the Davidic kingdom is being fulfilled now in part.

Prophecy—Truth which has been predicted and awaits fulfillment in the future.

Purgatory—The Roman Catholic Church's term describing the place where the dead go before they go to their eternal destiny.

Realized Millennialism—Preferred term of some amillennialists to describe their belief.

Reconstructionism—Belief that the church's task is to bring the world into conformity to the church. Places heavy stress upon reforming society.

Spiritualize—Applied to hermeneutics, it refers to giving a less than normal or literal interpretation to Scripture.

Soul Sleep—The condition that some believe occurs between death and resurrection.

Theology—From two Greek words meaning "God" and "word." Consists of various kinds of disciplines within the study of God and His Word.

Theological Covenants—Include the covenants of redemption, works, and grace. Contrasted with the biblical covenants described above.

Theonomy—Comes from two Greek words meaning "God" and "law." Stresses the need to bring the secular world under the jurisdiction of the Mosaic Law.

Traditionalism—Adherence to what has been believed in the past as opposed to new ideas and concepts.

Person Index

Subject Index

Scripture Index

About The Author

Robert P. Lightner, Th.D., is currently professor of systematic theology at Dallas Theological Seminary in Dallas, Texas. He has taught courses in Bible, theology, systematic theology and eschatology for thirty-seven years. He received a Th.B. from Baptist Bible Seminary, a Th.M. and Th.D. with honors from Dallas Theological Seminary, and an M.L.A. from Southern Methodist University.

He is listed in *Who's Who in American Education, Outstanding Educators of America,* and *Community Leaders of America.* Dr. Lightner is a member of the Pretribulation Study Group and the Grace Evangelical Society. He has authored numerous books and articles.

Dr. Lightner is married and has three daughters and ten grandchildren.